Merry Christmas   12/15/00

Dear,
    We hope you enjoy
reading and using this
book about angels!
        Love,
    Derald & Linda

A·N·G·E·L D·A·Y·S

Terry Lynn Taylor

A · N · G · E · L

A journal and daybook for everyone who walks with angels

D · A · Y · S

BALLANTINE BOOKS · NEW YORK

LIBRARY OF CONGRESS CATALOG CARD NUMBER: 95-94324
ISBN: 0-345-39160-8

Book design by Beth Tondreau Design / Robin Bentz

Manufactured in the United States of America
First Edition: July 1995

10   9   8   7   6   5   4   3   2   1

Contents

A·N·G·E·L D·A·Y·S

Introduction

*T*he angels are not a fad, or a trend, or a passing fancy. The popularity of angels reveals a change in consciousness that is touching the minds and hearts of many people. The angels are prevalent in the collective consciousness right now to help us keep beautiful human gifts from becoming extinct. The angels want us to keep our hearts in the right place and feed the world's soul with the arts of love, laughter, and grace, and with our natural creative energy. Regardless of how technologically organized the world may become, if we don't keep love and laughter alive, our souls and spirits will have nothing left to nourish them. This journal, one in which you rely on the angels for inspiration, can become a source of soul nourishment and spirit energy.

When we become aware of the love and guidance always available from the angels, our lives are transformed by an angelic uplifting of consciousness. Something actually changes in us and we feel and accept new impulses from life. Angels help us link our lives to Divine energy; they are messengers of light, who use the light to guide us. Angels are always nearby, ready to encourage us through inspiration, lighten our hearts, and remind us that where there is life there is joy.

Once you develop angel consciousness, you won't have to *believe* in the angels, because you will *know* them. You will be experiencing life with them. When you enter into angel consciousness, there will be no separation between an angel experience and a you experience. Angel consciousness is the awareness that you are a Divine being, and that you are guided by a higher wisdom in the Universe that operates for your greatest good. Most important, angel consciousness reminds us that life is meant to be enjoyed and lived, not suffered and endured.

Creating the Attitude of Angel Consciousness

Practice Gratitude

Being a living, breathing human is truly a miracle and a gift. Sometimes, though, life becomes full of stress and strain and we tend just to push through and neglect the here and now, especially if we perceive it to be full of painful observations. But the "here and now" is where our souls are known and accepted. It is where our spirits soar freely. The true way to live in continuous flow with the angels is to adopt the "gratitude attitude." When we are grateful to be alive the world no longer seems like a place of doom; it becomes a beautiful, unfolding landscape of Heaven. At those times when you feel that life has become overwhelming and exhausting, the best way to change this is to practice appreciation and gratitude.

Lighten Up

If you truly want to merge with the angels in your life, it is important that you take fun and humor *seriously*. We have a tendency to go through our time on earth with a heavy heart, forgetting to laugh and be joyful. Sometimes the best way to release a problem is to realize that in the scheme of the big picture our problems are really very small, and that we can change the chemistry of our problems by bringing the angels around for a good laugh. The angels want us to "get a life" and "get over it." This doesn't mean we carelessly disregard the painful issues in our lives, but simply that we don't let the heaviness rule our overall response to life. There is always time to take care of our pain and our issues, but it is important to understand that they are not what define us. Our pain is not who we are. We are interesting, complex beings who respond to life in a multitude of ways. Through the day we have several different emotional responses. Sometimes we feel angry and happy at the same time. Sometimes sadness comes upon us when we are basically joyful. We don't need to define ourselves by moods or emotions. Moods and emotions want to move on, they do not want to take up residence in our minds. Let the changing landscape of your heart and mind move and change like the passing clouds that create beautiful angel art in the sky above.

Understand the Quickening Energy

Many people feel that the energy, or pace, of the world—the planet, the Universe—has sped up. We hear talk of instant manifestation and instant karma. I have experienced this quickening energy and I have found it chaotic at times. As the feeling of chaos is not particularly pleasant, I have learned that I must center myself in the here and now. We are told that the Earth is rotating constantly, yet we do not feel the sensation of it because we are *on* the Earth and *in* the experience. So to deal with the quickening energy we must be in the energy, we must embrace it. When we can center ourselves, we are able to use the quickened energy to manifest what we need in our lives to be our best selves.

Seek Truth and Beauty in Writing
"Beauty is truth, truth beauty,"—that is all
Ye know on earth, and all ye need to know.—John Keats

Writing is one of those natural human activities that have been compromised by strict rules, comparisons, criticisms, and fears. Most of us went through schooling to learn to read and write. And most of our learning and assignments required that we write words down on paper. I propose that, regardless of your preconceived notions of what a writer is, you become a writer in your own right. There is a writer in you, because if you think and feel, and talk, then you can write. Writing, like any other craft, gets better and easier the more often you do it. As you get to know yourself better and more fully, your writing will reflect your new depth and wisdom. When you come to the point of accepting yourself and your life—who knows the levels you can reach? The possibilities are endless, especially if you are living in angel consciousness.

If you start out writing to become famous or to make money, you will take yourself down some futile paths, regardless of any success you acquire. When something is not truth, or is not you, or is not from your heart, it will not carry the essence of beauty, and therefore will not last in the hearts and minds of humanity. Uta Hagan, the master acting teacher, once said, "Love the art in yourself, not yourself in the art." You must love writing for its own sake. You must write for the sake of expressing what is deep and true inside of you. Use truth and beauty as guides for your art and allow your passion to grow and motivate you.

When you *try* to be clever in your writing, or *try* to be creative or to have an interesting "style," you'll miss the mark. Trying is not doing and when you have something to write, you have something to say, so say it and don't worry about style or creative twist—that will come naturally. Creative cleverness comes from a higher plane of imagination that can only be reached if you are not *trying* or *spending* effort. Creativity happens when you get "flow" happening. Flow happens more readily with practice and doing.

The Art of Journal Healing

"Writing makes a map, and there is something about a journey that begs to have its passage marked."—Christina Baldwin, *Life's Companion*

Each of our lives is a special journey of healing, questioning, learning, loving, creating, knowing ourselves, and making peace with our choices. A journey denotes travel from one place to another. Our lives are pathways, spiritual journeys. The spiritual traveling we do is in our minds and hearts. We may never leave our houses, but we can still travel very far on our paths.

The true definition of healing is to make whole. To become whole, we must live with our entire being: body, mind, spirit, and soul. It is not easy to know our souls and to listen to our hearts. It takes practice and the desire, plus the courage to venture into the unknown parts of ourselves. Keeping a journal is one of the best ways available for getting in touch with who you are, at the many levels on which you exist and respond. Keeping a journal is about discovering the true story of your life.

Consciousness is far more than a waking, physical response. We hear, see, feel, absorb, and record much more information than we are actually aware of. In our dreams we go into a whole other realm, in which the physical body is asleep but the consciousness experiences myriad sensations. Our waking decisions may seem to be very linear, logical expressions we put forth, yet we are really guided by a higher point of reference that knows the future, the present, and the past. Our actual decisions and responses to life often have very little to do with our narrowly focused logic. We have all looked back on circumstances in our lives and seen how they evolved in a purposeful way that had very little to do with what we thought we were creating or deciding. This is what is so exciting about having a spiritual response to life with the angels as our companions and creative partners. When we record our lives in our journals, we will witness miracles that we might otherwise have missed.

Keeping a journal will help you feel spiritually centered in the here and now. It will also help you to be with your pain or discomfort in the here and now. When we stay with, rather than avoid, our pain and suffering, and get to know these feelings, we forge a new part of ourselves that rides the pain like a wave. As the wave recedes, it makes way for the next one, which may bring joy or comfort. Waves of pain must go on, and when we acknowledge them with truth, we transform the pain itself into hope and even joy. Keeping a journal helps us grow the new limb that automatically reaches out to the angels for support in facing fear and pain with truth.

Keeping an Angel Journal

I no longer have the time to write in my journal for long periods of time each day, but I still want to keep track of my goals, emotions, feelings, and impressions, to take time for some self-reflection, to understand the outer seasonal forces, and to pay attention to the angels in my life. If you feel that you don't have much time to write each day but that you would like to record similar hopes and contemplations, then this journal is for you. The first book I wrote, *Messengers of Light*, came from my journals. The moment the angels became a guiding light on my spiritual path, I took note in my journal. If the angels are just beginning to dance in your consciousness your journal will be a way to let the relationship grow and flourish, a way to discover the wonderful ways life changes when you acknowledge that the angels are always with you.

The concept for this particular journal comes from my own needs. For years I have been imagining the perfect journal that would allow me to keep track of myself each day in a simple way and to notice and integrate the seasonal influences in an organized way. Knowing what is happening in the hemisphere where we live and respecting the energy influence of the reigning seasonal archangel encourages freedom, creativity, and increased "success" in life.

An angel journal needs to be fun and simple to keep, providing a place where we develop a deeper personal connection with the angels. The goal here is to take life as lightly as the angels do. This journal is designed to keep the angels close to our hearts. It is a personal journal and daily guide for lighthearted communion with the angels. If you spend just a few minutes in the early morning and late evening with this journal and take the time to keep up with what is happening in your life, you will be surprised at the increase in your level of self-awareness and transcendence. You will also come to understand how to influence your own life with your highest inner motivations and to live under the law of grace.

When the angels become an everyday part of our lives, keeping a daily journal helps our angelic awareness remain alive and strong. Taking the time to reflect each day on angelic love gives life a heavenly glow. We become keenly aware of our own guardian angels and the other angels who help us through the year. We discover that there is an abundance of blessings to be grateful for. Most of all, we bring the wonderful qualities of angel consciousness into our way of life, increasing our capacity for having fun. Fun is important, it is a need we never outgrow. But the things that create fun change and we must continue to discover what brings us fun and enjoyment—another good reason for keeping a journal.

Seasonal influence

Paying attention to seasonal influence assists us in discovering and developing our own innate creative gifts. The seasons guide us on an inner and outer level. Each season is ruled by one of the four chief arch-angels: Michael rules autumn, Gabriel lights the winter, Raphael orchestrates spring, and Uriel directs the summer. During each arch-angel's reign he focuses his unique light into our lives, so that we can use the energies of the season for our highest good. By paying close at-tention to the seasonal influence you will know when to slow down for a while and let the ethers imprint a change on your being. We have cycles of creativity, and the more we pay attention to the angels and the seasons, the purer our creative energy will flow. It is important to understand what happens to us in each season, so that we don't de-spair. Paying attention to the seasonal influence and what it means to you each day can help you bring the sacred into the present.

Because this is a journal that you can begin at any point in the year, it is up to you to find the information on the season that is in progress as you start your journal and to take note of what is happen-ing outside your door.

The seasonal information which precedes the writing pages can increase your awareness of what to look for, tell you what seasonal festivals occur, and suggest specific thoughts to ponder during the sea-son. The ruling archangel is introduced and key words that bring the season's spirit alive are listed. For a more in-depth spiritual understanding of seasonal influence, I have provided a list of books in the back of the journal.

How to Use the Writing Pages

The writing pages are organized by week and each week includes four pages. An *angelic spirit of the week* guides each week's writing. The first page for each week provides a space for jotting down *goals*; *prayer requests* or notes to your highest angel; *concerns* or worries to solve creatively with the angels during the week or stresses to avoid; names of particular *angels to call on* and *people who need special blessings*; comments inspired by your *seasonal awareness*. The week starts with Sunday and ends with Saturday, and a final space is provided each week for noting things that inspired *gratitude*, how the angels helped or made themselves known during the week, and the overall feelings of the week. You can use this space for closure of the week if desired.

Angelic spirit of the week

For each week there is a spirit or essence to explore. Some of the spirit focuses have contemplations written as an affirmation, others provide things to think about or accomplish. Basically this information is just a little nudge for increased angel awareness and food for thought. It is so important that we really *think* each day, that we take our thoughts a little farther down the line while looking for new questions to keep us keenly interested in life. Feeling young at heart comes from questioning and allowing a healthy curiosity about how to do life well.

Listing goals

A goal is an objective, something we hope to achieve, reach, or capture. It is important that we approach our goals without creating limits. If we get too attached to a narrow definition of what we perceive our goals to be, we may miss the angels' efforts to affect and guide our quests, thus losing the opportunity to enhance our goals. The angels don't want us to concentrate on our goals to the exclusion of all else, but to focus on what we have and do in the moment. While it is important to have desires, dreams, wishes, and destinations, it is equally important to avoid being weighed down by them.

When sending energy toward a goal, be sure to examine your underlying intent. Also, when defining goals, remember that "everything is subject to *changels*"—"changels" are angels of change, and life is change. When the angels become part of our lives, our goals and desires can become transcendent.

Prayer requests: writing notes to the angels

Prayer is communication of our highest desires. It is a creative way to express ourselves to God. The angels carry our prayers to God. They do not want us praying to them but to the Great Creator. The angels can be thought of as our prayer partners. Prayer links our souls, minds, and hearts up to the ultimate source of love and abundance in the Universe. Prayer is a powerful spiritual tool, perhaps the only way to bring about change. The purpose of prayer is to seek the highest good of all concerned.

Writing notes to the angels is a fun way to learn about ourselves and what we desire. Use this space to communicate to the Highest Source of light in the Universe. Write a note to your angels, to the angels of others, or to the angel of a group or situation. Special requests may range from immediate tasks to long-range goals. The key is the action of asking and the involvement, and purification, of your intent.

Acknowledging what brings stress, concern, and worry

There is a space in this journal to write down your concerns, including those things that cause stress, anxiety, and fear. Fear can be one of our best teachers if we handle it properly. We can miss a lot in life when we worry too much. When we take the time to identify the sources of fears and worries, we initiate the desire to change. Don't allow fear to paralyze you. Ask the angels for help. By tracking your worries, you can look back on them at a later date and see how real they were, and notice any patterns that need reworking. Use this section to identify what weights you down. Once you know what is upsetting, you can choose to change it.

Angels to call on; people to bless

A central part of our lives is our relationship with others. When we are concerned about others, it helps to bless them and send them light and angels. This space is for doing that and for calling on specific angels to come and help you in your life.

Seasonal awareness

This space is for you to record pertinent information about cosmic influences, ideas for holiday angelic celebrations, any significant event for the week, things to look for in nature (for example, birds nesting), and special nature moments such as spectacular sunrises.

Daily reflection

There is not enough room to write a huge amount each day in the space provided for reflection. That is intentional. This is a space for capturing the essence of what you are bringing to the day. If you want to keep writing on, then have a notebook nearby to continue your writing. One way to use the daily reflection space is to review your goals, concerns, the weekly spirit, and any issues in the forefront of your mind. If you'd like, go into a short meditation. After you meditate, write down a few thoughts and feelings.

Another way of reflection is simply to contemplate your day and life in the morning and write down any thoughts or feelings that need to be expressed. In the morning, you may want to record a dream you had; in the evening you can go over your day, let go of that which didn't go well, and concentrate on what went well. Create a little ritual each morning with your journal and spend special time with it. Get up a little earlier if you need to; the sleep you lose will be replaced by the peace of knowing yourself a little better and starting your day out the angels' way. In the evening, take the time to reflect on your day. Instead of watching the news before bed, which is rarely a lift in consciousness, take out your journal and go over your own "news."

Or, write about your upcoming day, including positive results and events you would like to see come about.

Get into the spirit of angel journaling and allow yourself a certain self-indulgence. (I would never suggest self-indulgence at any other time; in fact, it's best to leave indulgence behind when you enter the outside world.) Fall in love with the process of writing, develop a passion for knowing who you are on paper. Don't get caught up in judging how you write. Simply love doing it. Record your own truth and beauty without worrying about rules.

Just remember that this is your time and it is fun time. Don't think of journaling as something you *have to do*, but something you look forward to doing. It doesn't take discipline once you decide you like it, and you *will* like it when you get your daily ritual going. Once you notice that the angels are enjoying your daily reflection with you, all kinds of wonders will take place. You will begin truly to know the world as a magical place. Your experience of life is all that matters in the end. Our experiences are the only things we can keep with us. Life asks us to experience it, not just think it or daydream it.

I have suggested uses for this journal, but my hope is that you will be creative and use it in whatever way you want. Take the time to express who you are. Take the time to *know* who you are. Life is not a rehearsal. This is the real thing. Right now you are alive—full of spirit, passion, and creative energy that is always waiting for the chance to release magic into your life.

Seasonal Information

*E*ven though the calendar year starts in January, from a spiritual perspective the year begins in autumn. The four distinct seasons of the year relate to the honoring of specific positions of the sun in relationship to the Earth. *Equinox* refers to either of the two times in the year—in spring and fall—when day and night are of equal length. It is a point of balance. *Solstice* means sun standing still. It, too, occurs twice a year, when the sun is farthest from the equator. These solar transition points determine the changeovers of active influences, and also cause us to be aware that each season is Divinely watched over by a particular archangel.

A·U·T·U·M·N

AUTUMNAL EQUINOX

September 22–23

RULING ARCHANGEL

Michael

ELEMENT

Air

ENERGY DIRECTION

West

KEY WORDS AND THOUGHTS

Harvest, the fall from childhood innocence, preparing for winter, initiation, innocence into experience, adolescence, self-discipline, awareness of what is good for the whole, come in from the garden, fruits become seeds, service, healing, teaching, reaping benefits of growth, maturity, goals, indication of the gifts you will have in winter, silent wisdom, death, intense inner work, inner resources to prepare for the future, calm on the surface, intense underneath, time to harvest and purify.

*A*ir is the element of autumn and the element of the mind. Archangel Michael and his angels renew the mind with the highest Divine light.

Michael's name means "one who is like God." Michael is the archangel of autumn, and the warrior and protector of all that is good. The time of Michael begins September 23 and concludes on the winter solstice, December 21. During these days we can more deeply experience the angelic presence of Michael.

As it opens, September points to cultural shifts occurring with Labor Day and the acknowledgment that a new year of learning has begun. We can realize that a special time to deepen our spiritual lives has approached with the end of summer and the arriving energies of Archangel Michael in late September.

The Archangel Michael is responsible for the expansion of human consciousness. He urges individual humans to find freedom within their own Christ consciousness through Divine love. The Archangel Michael protects the spark of pure God, the Christ consciousness, in our soul. Michael is usually shown in pictures clad in armor, with a shield and weapon, taming the dragon of evil intentions. He is the angel who cleanses persons of discord and evil; in other words he is the angel offering protective light that will shield us from negative forces. Michael brings us courage to see the light of truth and offers comfort in adversity. A color frequently associated with Michael is vivid blue. Michael imparts God-ideas and initiative to humans and is the greatest angel of protection.

Angelologist K. Martin-Kuri explains, "Michael accepts it as fact that humanity has taken possession of its own intelligence, either for good or for purposes of hindrance. It is after all through this sense of free thinking that our world progresses, or retrogrades. Michael would have humanity exercise this intelligence and freedom with a sense of profound responsibility toward the Universe and toward the heavenly powers."

SEASONAL IDEAS AND THOUGHTS FOR MICHAEL DAYS

- As summertime ends and activities become more centered around work, school, or accomplishments, use the precious transition time in September before the Feast of Michael on the twenty-ninth to *eliminate* all that has become unproductive and useless in your life. Let this be a time of shedding the old skins of your inner life.

- Sit down with paper and pen and focus on that which you need to strengthen and improve in your life. Analyze what the obstacles have been and proceed to transform them through plans for inner change and new action. Most people are accustomed to doing this kind of shift in their lives during January, but the most angelically supportive time to do it is as we enter the fall. For then the forces of Archangel Michael will be available to help penetrate areas of darkness—areas of concern that need improvement—and transform them into areas of light.
- Think seriously about the global civilization that extends beyond individual nations. Be aware of how your own actions affect the whole family of humanity.
- Find new areas of your life that will increase inner freedom. This does not mean lack of responsibility, but a more open way of thinking, a new line of intelligence.
- Value the protection of the angels in your life and know that Michael is your warrior against spiritual darkness. Hold in your mind the picture of Michael conquering the dragon.
- Make this a time to forgive yourself and others for the past.
- Think of the power of faith to overcome dark areas of your life and fill them with light.
- Honor the angels, who never seek anything for themselves while serving the good in us.

- Keep in mind that angels do not belong to any one
  religion; they go beyond a single religion.
  The angels represent the Divine energy of God.

MICHAEL'S OCCASIONS TO HONOR

Michaelmas: September 29

Into the darkness comes the light of God.

Feast of the Guardian Angels: October 2

God's love shines down to us through his angels.

Feast of Saint Francis: October 4

By the power of faith, all is possible.

Feast of All Saints: November 1

Each of us has a saint within. Let your saint appear.

Thanksgiving

A day to honor the selfless love of your guardian angel.

Immaculate Conception: December 8

Purity of heart is the start of all Holy deeds.

Remember to let autumn be the time to shed the old ways of thinking, feeling, and acting. Prepare to receive the renewing blessings of
Gabriel that start on December 21 and extend to the spring equinox.

W·I·N·T·E·R

WINTER SOLSTICE

December 21

RULING ARCHANGEL

Gabriel

ELEMENT

Earth

ENERGY DIRECTION

North

KEY WORDS AND THOUGHTS

*I nner light, revelation, maturity, responsibility,
acceptance, inner peace, comfort, generosity of soul,
time for new initiatives, forgiveness of ourselves and
others, ancestors, ancient memories of
God, meditation, reflection,
heavenly tasks.*

*A*s daylight is reduced to its lowest amount on December 21 a very special doorway to inner light opens. This is the time when rays of spiritual blessing and love can enter our lives. We have the opportunity to receive inspiration at this time of year, if we choose to make the time from late December to March 21 the most inward journey, the deepest inner work. Nature helps us in this time of reflection. The colder weather encourages you to draw into your *self*, to set boundaries, to limit unnecessary actions. It is a wonderful time to study spiritual matters, to deepen the devotional life. As you celebrate various holidays, know that each one opens the door further to let the light of Heaven enter your life in a personal way.

Winter is the time of love and of taking the light within. Earth is the element of winter, and Archangel Gabriel and his angels bring us the potential for peace and harmony on Earth. The Archangel Gabriel's influence can be felt during the wintertime in many wonderful and meaningful ways. The time of Gabriel begins on the winter solstice, December 21, takes us through the winter holidays, and culminates with the spring celebrations of Passover and Easter.

Gabriel is heaven's favored messenger, the one who announced to Mary, Queen of the Angels, that she would be the mother of Christ.

This is a season in which to prepare for inner revelation from your own angels and to think upon the meaning of birthing the highest consciousness within yourself.

Gabriel's name means "the strength of God" or "God is my strength." Gabriel is most often depicted holding a lily, which represents purity. One of Gabriel's tasks is to encourage the purity of souls. A lily is also a symbol of the Immaculate Conception. According to tradition, when the apostles opened Mary's coffin, only lilies were found. Gabriel's color is white or crystal, and he represents purity and resurrection.

In *The Blessed Angels*, Manly P. Hall says this about Gabriel: "In art this archangel is presented as a graceful being with a beautiful face and head and a flame-like curl of hair above the forehead. His attributes are a lily and a scroll inscribed with 'Ave Maria Gratia Plena.' He is sometimes shown with a scepter or an olive branch as a symbol of peace on earth. On January 12, 1951, Pope Pius XII declared Gabriel to be patron of those involved in electronic communication, television, telephone, and telegraph, thus emphasizing Gabriel's function as a messenger."

SEASONAL IDEAS AND THOUGHTS FOR GABRIEL DAYS

- Winter is the best time to connect with the Divine Feminine mysteries, the Mary impulse, and to meditate upon the things that Mary experienced.
- Think about whether you are prepared to receive the word—the message—of the angels.
- Use this season as a time for deepening your inner holiness.
- Design activities that will bring forth a new level of purity in all you do, think, and feel.
- Expand your devotional life and do research on the lives of Jesus Christ, the prophets, and Buddha. These beings are very important to the angels.
- When you receive a gift, think of the spiritual message connected to it. Be alert as never before. The angels are glad to participate in your understanding by helping others present you with loving gifts. If someone gives you a fragile golden leaf left over from autumn, see that there is a message in it from the heavens.
- Approach the holiday season with an awareness of the world of the angels. They are preparing us each year for this inner work, and it is up to us to make the season truly Holy instead of just an open space on our calendars.

- Set patterns and begin to think of the seeds you want to plant in the Spring.

GABRIEL'S OCCASIONS TO HONOR

Hanukkah

The light of God shall triumph.

Christmas Eve: December 24

It is the Divine Feminine that brings forth the Christ within.

Christmas Days: December 25 to January 6

Holy days to meet with the Christ Being in a personal way.

Epiphany: January 6

Honor the wisdom and gifts of the ancients and receive the Son of God.

Annunciation by Gabriel: March 25

I will do whatever the heavens ask of me.

Ash Wednesday

It is a serious time to prepare spiritually.

Palm Sunday

The process begins.

Passover

The darkness shall pass by because of God's mercy.

Easter

From out of loving sacrifice, great light emerges.

S · P · R · I · N · G

VERNAL EQUINOX

March 20–21

RULING ARCHANGEL

Raphael

ELEMENT

Fire

ENERGY DIRECTION

East

KEY WORDS AND THOUGHTS

Emergence, awakening, the newly born, illumination, expansion, surging, the light brings vision, new beginnings, enthusiasm, energy turns from internal to external, joy, resurrection, hope, opportunity for a new path, move life upward. Like the seed burst open to release aspiring life, spring brings to Earth the forces of growth and renewal.

*S*pring fever is a real, physical phenomenon that affects everyone in some way each spring. There are actually chemical changes that take place in our systems, due to awakening hormones that trigger increased activity. All the new colors, scents, sounds, and light bombard our minds and overload our senses so that many of us get a light-headed, giddy feeling. Think about what other force makes us feel light and giddy and heightens our sense of beauty. You guessed it—the angels. Springtime is one big angel experience.

The day of the spring equinox is nature's message of balance, for on this day there are equal times of daylight and darkness creating a momentary balance of day and night. We must remember that we are coming from a time of hibernation and our minds and bodies must be prepared for the energy surge of spring, when the daylight hours will take the lead and the darkness will fade. To utilize the energy of spring we must stay balanced and centered. Desires and energies begin to surge, like the sap rising in a tree. Pay attention to purification, and purify your desires and energies, so that you can use the creative fire for the highest good of all concerned—especially yourself. Fire is spring's element, so be careful not to get burned, or burned out.

Raphael's healing influence is most noticeable on Earth through the beauty of nature. Raphael is frequently associated with the color green. Through the greening of spring, Raphael brings humanity Divine impulses for consecration: healing, science, truth, and life in harmony with the beauty of nature. Raphael heals the soul and helps guide its development.

In *Angels: An Endangered Species*, Malcolm Godwin describes Raphael as: "both the chummiest and funniest of all the angelic flock and . . . often depicted chatting merrily with some unsuspecting mortal. His sunny disposition is possibly due to his being Regent, or Angel of the Sun." Raphael is not as intense as the other archangels and wants us to enjoy springtime. You can imagine that he dwells on the Earth during spring, and that he will respond to your thoughts of new growth in your soul.

In her book *Star Gates*, Corinne Heline tells of a legend about Raphael: "Each eventide Raphael gathers up all prayers for healing which have arisen from mankind during the day and carries them up into heaven, where as he presents them before the throne of God, they are transformed into fragrant blossoms, which are then borne down to earth by his serving Angels to bring solace and comfort wherever there is pain and sorrow."

Following a season of inner work and learning, a restlessness comes upon the soul with the stirrings of new growth, new awareness, and new abilities beginning to manifest. This is the wonderful activity of the Archangel Raphael, whose presence can be felt with the new sense of health and well-being that streams into our bodies and our minds with the bursting out of spring. Raphael's name means "God has healed" or "the Shining One who heals." The Archangel Raphael and his ministering angels set out to heal through balance and to create beauty that reflects the love of God.

SEASONAL IDEAS AND THOUGHTS FOR
RAPHAEL DAYS

- During this season, strive for balance in all areas of your life. As new growth appears in nature, reflect upon the harmony of the masculine and feminine energies that created the new seeds. Hold the image of new spiritual growth that you have received during the winter, and protect it until it becomes strong.
- This is a time to nurture the impulses of new wisdom entering your life. It is a good time to write about these perceptions.
- Honor the growth of spiritual light in others, and express your awareness to them.

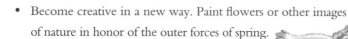

- Become creative in a new way. Paint flowers or other images of nature in honor of the outer forces of spring.
- Allow feelings of joy and freedom to lift your soul during spring, while remaining connected to your daily life and its responsibilities. There can be no new branches on a tree without new roots as well.
- Focus on healing your *relationships* as well as yourself, with the help of Raphael and the healing angels.
- Do a mental and physical spring cleaning. Put things into order and harmony.
- Release and express your Divine spark into a new creation or project.
- Celebrate spring with the angels and bring Heaven to Earth in your personal environment. Keep a mental image of Heaven when you listen to the birds and ask the angels for a sample of this sound in the Heaven realm. When you look at a flower, watch the colors expand and let the fragrance intoxicate your mind as if the angels have lifted you into Heaven. Ask the angels to heighten your perception—absorb spring's beauty into your soul. Pretty soon you will realize that Heaven is here with us on Earth and we can attract glimpses of the angelic realm whenever we want.

RAPHAEL'S OCCASIONS TO HONOR

Buddha's Birthday

Through wisdom and into Love I shall walk my path.

S·U·M·M·E·R

SUMMER SOLSTICE

June 21

RULING ARCHANGEL

Uriel

ELEMENT

Water

ENERGY DIRECTION

South

KEY WORDS AND THOUGHTS

The outer world reveals itself, flowers become fruits, tentative to definite, reaching goals, truths manifest, outward light, naked self, faeries and nature spirits, dancing, dreamtime.

*S*ummer's force is light, the Holy radiant light of the sun and all its blessings of fruition. When summer comes, life is full, the sun reaches its zenith and its full power is manifest. Summer is a truly creative time: fruits are ripening, vegetables are maturing, and the trees give their welcome shade. In the springtime, the blossoms intoxicated us with the rich blessings of things to come. Now blossoms have given way to fruit and the scent is pure sweetness. The creative forces of the Divine Cosmic Feminine are upon us during summer. Love, music, festivals, and dance are in order. The summer is yours. It is a gift. When you feel the warmth of the sun and smell the sweet air, stop and thank the angels for the blessings.

Uriel is the archangel of devotional worship, ministration, and peace. His name means "fire of God" (some interpret it to mean "God is light"), and colors frequently associated with him are gold and ruby. Usually shown with a scroll, he inspires the prophets and conveys ideas to teachers. He is sometimes represented as the angel who wrestled Jacob. With his angels of ministry he restores salvation and sanity in spiritual emergencies.

With the approach of summer, and the Festival of the Sun on June 21, the abundant greenery and flowering of nature gently pulls us

out into the sunshine. A major shift draws us outward and off to play, to vacation, and to be with friends. This is important because the time we spend focusing on the outer world of nature and friends creates a balance with the inner work that has been
accomplished since the last autumn. Archangel Uriel has a wonderful impulse that leads us to reveal the truth; and summer is a good time of year to observe how we do this in various ways. Think of the almost-nude bodies in swimming attire, the ease with which we accept someone in very casual attire, perspiring from the heat. And we become extremely interested in what we eat during the summer. Working in a garden becomes a grounding thing to do. Focusing on the gorgeous colors of fresh fruits and vegetables that predominate in summertime meals gives us a true appreciation of the abundance nature provides us.

Our works through the year that have been inward now need to become outward. Uriel warns us that we must always have a balance between ideals and the manifestation of those ideals. With Uriel nothing can be kept hidden. As a teaching archangel, he will cause us to reveal our true being; thus, we must try to reconcile the inner and outer life.

The summer season begins with the longest day of the year, a time to honor the sun. This is also the Feast of Saint John the Baptist and, in some traditions, the day the Christmas tree is burned in a special fire. This means we can let the sun burn away any debris that stands in the way of our learning to create with the angels. It is a time to reflect on spiritual baptism and what this means. Creativity is essential at this season, as we use our free will to serve the heavens in the outer world.

SEASONAL IDEAS AND THOUGHTS FOR URIEL DAYS

- During summer, focus a little more on larger issues that affect us globally and nationally. It is good for our attention to go beyond our personal lives.
- When we prepare our fresh vegetables with love, an extra dash of healing energy will be present in our food.
- Seek reconciliation with those who have harmed you or whom you have harmed.
- Plan new ways to express your delight and gratitude for the help of the angels.
- Use this season as a time to paint, create music, and write. Expand your creative horizon in everything you do.
- Get enough rest in preparation for the inner work of the autumn season. Hold off on deep reading or spiritual study for autumn and enjoy

the summer Earth forces that pull your attention outward.

- Remember, winter is the in-breath for your soul, a time to receive; summer is out-breath—a time to give.
- Rejoice over achievements of a spiritual nature that have become reflected in the outer world of your life.
- Uncover your real essence, become more truly who you are. Be true to yourself.
- Think of the spiritual purposes behind the establishment of each nation.

URIEL'S OCCASIONS TO HONOR

Saint John's festival: June 21

Let the fire of God baptize your soul.

Feast of Peter and Paul: June 29

Be at one with your commitment to God.

Yom Kippur

Today I forgive my enemies and myself.

Rosh Hashana

A celebration of the new impulses in my life.

MOON

*T*he new moon rises with the sun and is in the same astrological sign as the sun as it begins the lunar month. The new moon can be seen as a thin crescent right after the sun sets a few days after the official new moon. As the new moon starts its cycle it is referred to as the waxing or increasing moon, and is seen as the "right-hand moon." If you put your right hand out in front of you, the thumb and index finger make a curve in line with the new crescent moon. The waning, decreasing moon is seen as the "left-hand moon."

The moon cycle is divided into quarters, or phases, the first being the new moon. The second quarter is the point halfway between the new moon and the full moon. The half-moon rises around noon and sets around midnight, and is seen in the sky during the first half of the night. The third quarter brings the full moon, when the moon and the sun are opposite one another and the moon can reflect the full light of the sun. The full moon makes a spectacular entrance into the sky at sunset. As the moon wanes, it enters the fourth quarter, halfway between full and new again. The waning moon enters the sky at midnight and fades in the zenith as the sun rises. The new moon is a time of peace and beginnings. The full moon is a time of manifestation and harvest.

DAYS OF THE WEEK

*J*ust as the seasons and the moon affect our daily lives, so too do the days of the week.
You should be aware of the following attributes associated with each day.

SUNDAY *The sun's day, Michael's day: fire, masculine energy, mental processes, drastic purification, joy, success, growth*

MONDAY *The moon's day: water, feminine energy, intuitive processes, healing, nurturing, fertility, cycles, inspiration, emotions, psychic impressions*

TUESDAY *Tyr's (Mars's) day: spirit of justice, athletics, war, law, discipline and integrity, peacekeeping, spiritual warriorship*

WEDNESDAY *Raphael's (Mercury's) day: poetic inspiration, ecstasy, wisdom, communication, search for knowledge, muse, ingenuity*

THURSDAY *Thor's (Jupiter's) day: god of thunder, contracts, commitments, strength, protection, order, expansiveness, optimism, mercy, generosity, success*

FRIDAY *Freya's (Venus's) day: goddess of love and beauty, feeling, wildness, romance, creativity, harmony, arts, crafts, fertility*

SATURDAY *Saturn's day: Father Time, god of old age and decay, limitations overcome, alternative realities, discipline, spiritual lessons, clarity of intention*

ANGELIC SPIRIT

FOR

FIFTY-TWO

WEEKS

ANGELIC SPIRIT OF THE WEEK

Gratitude

Gratitude is our most direct line to God and the angels. If we take the time, no matter how crazy and troubled we feel, we can find something to be thankful for. The more we *seek* gratitude, the more reason the angels will give us for gratitude and joy to exist in our lives.

CONTEMPLATION

*I shall wake up with a song of gratitude in
my heart.
I will thank the angels for the miraculous process
of life
that I notice vibrating all around me.
I am glad to be alive, I feel blessed by the angels each day.
I am honored to be a human at this crucial time in the
history of humanity.
Thank you God.*

Goals:

Prayer requests
or notes to your
highest angel:

Concerns, worries,
fears to overcome:

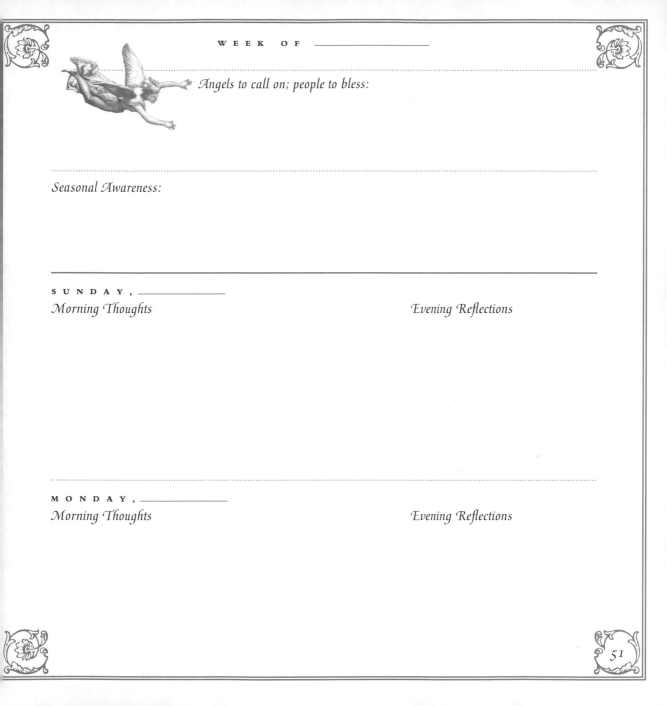

WEEK OF _____

Angels to call on; people to bless:

Seasonal Awareness:

SUNDAY, _____

Morning Thoughts   *Evening Reflections*

MONDAY, _____

Morning Thoughts   *Evening Reflections*

TUESDAY, _____

Morning Thoughts   *Evening Reflections*

WEDNESDAY, _____

Morning Thoughts   *Evening Reflections*

THURSDAY, _____

Morning Thoughts   *Evening Reflections*

FRIDAY, _____
Morning Thoughts   *Evening Reflections*

SATURDAY, _____
Morning Thoughts   *Evening Reflections*

Thoughts About the Week:

Transformation

A spiritual transformation brings a time when you assess your values and start living in full integrity. Many people have experiences that change their lives and send them searching for deeper values and deeper spiritual knowledge. It doesn't matter what sends you searching deeper; the experiences can range from near-death experiences and angelic intervention in emergencies, to watching a movie, reading a book, or meeting an interesting person.

WHAT ARE YOUR VALUES?

Our core values probably won't change much through life; however, our moment-to-moment guiding values may change many times depending on our awareness and the situation. When our hearts and minds awaken to the universal truth, our values will deepen and life will become meaningful. Making honorable choices without compromising our core values becomes paramount on the angel pathway.

Goals:

*Prayer requests
or notes to your
highest angel:*

*Concerns, worries,
fears to overcome:*

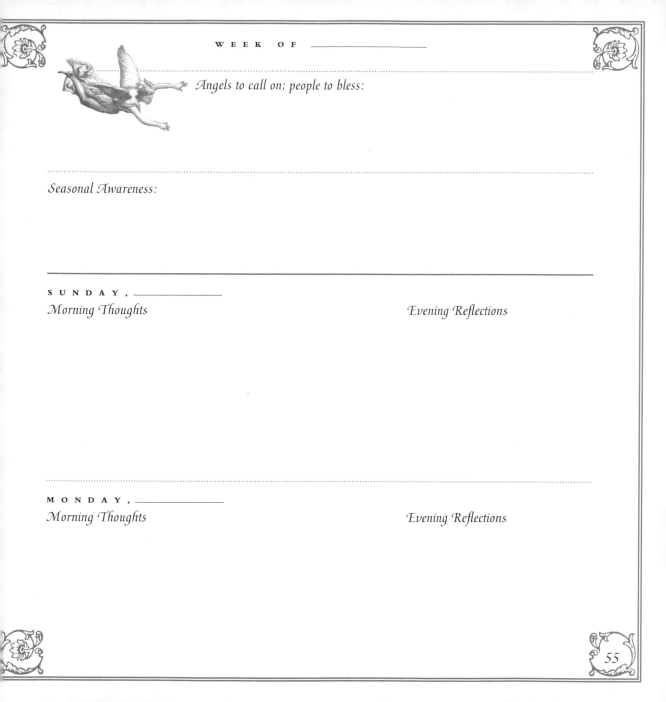

WEEK OF _____

Angels to call on; people to bless:

Seasonal Awareness:

SUNDAY, _____

Morning Thoughts   *Evening Reflections*

MONDAY, _____

Morning Thoughts   *Evening Reflections*

TUESDAY, _____

Morning Thoughts   *Evening Reflections*

WEDNESDAY, _____

Morning Thoughts   *Evening Reflections*

THURSDAY, _____

Morning Thoughts   *Evening Reflections*

FRIDAY, _____
Morning Thoughts   *Evening Reflections*

SATURDAY, _____
Morning Thoughts   *Evening Reflections*

Thoughts About the Week:

Courage

Courage does not mean conquering fear as much as it means integrating real passion into our lives. Courage gives us inner strength to live passionately. Living passionately gives us a deeper love of life; but when we love deeply, fear can present our biggest obstacle. When we have fears (of loss, of suffering, and of death) we know we have a deep connection to life. The key is to use our courage to see that the time spent fearing is worse than that which we fear. Ultimately, if we have consciously accepted the angels into our lives, fear has less room to roam.

CONTEMPLATION

Danger is only a chance of harm.
When I sense danger I know I have
the courage to face it with truth.
Fear is not my partner in life.
I ask the angels to come closer
and guide me beyond fear to a deeper knowing.
Courage warms my soul and lights the darkness.
Nothing can stop the light.

Goals:

Prayer requests
or notes to your
highest angel:

Concerns, worries,
fears to overcome:

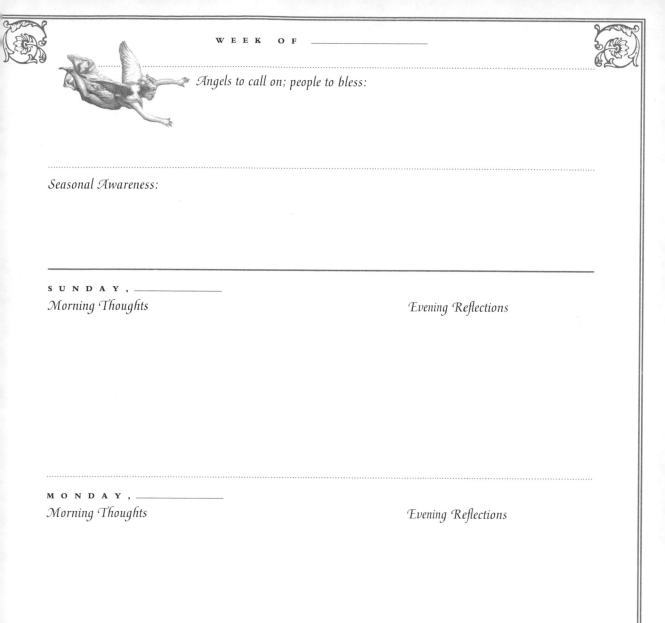

Angels to call on; people to bless:

Seasonal Awareness:

SUNDAY, _____

Morning Thoughts   *Evening Reflections*

MONDAY, _____

Morning Thoughts   *Evening Reflections*

TUESDAY, _____

Morning Thoughts   *Evening Reflections*

WEDNESDAY, _____

Morning Thoughts   *Evening Reflections*

THURSDAY, _____

Morning Thoughts   *Evening Reflections*

FRIDAY, _____
Morning Thoughts   *Evening Reflections*

SATURDAY, _____
Morning Thoughts   *Evening Reflections*

Thoughts About the Week:

Evolution

Humans are designed to evolve; it is programmed in our cells. To evolve is to develop or work out, and comes from the Latin word *evolvere*, which means to unroll. We were rolled up in the womb and our lives are a process of revealing and unveiling what we were protecting in the womb—our spirits. To evolve also implies getting better and improving through trial and error. The angels protect our souls and spirits while we evolve our minds upward and outward.

OUR VEHICLE OF EVOLUTION
IS THE PERSON THAT
WE WERE BORN AS

We each have to face our personal evolution and to realize that we are part of the larger evolution of humanity. Both are equally important, and each one supports the other. Spiritual evolution requires personal choices that lead to the betterment of the whole. Evolution that leads to the Divine light is a noble choice and demands that we trust that things are getting better and will continue to expand in love. Evolve with the angels.

Goals:

*Prayer requests
or notes to your
highest angel:*

*Concerns, worries,
fears to overcome:*

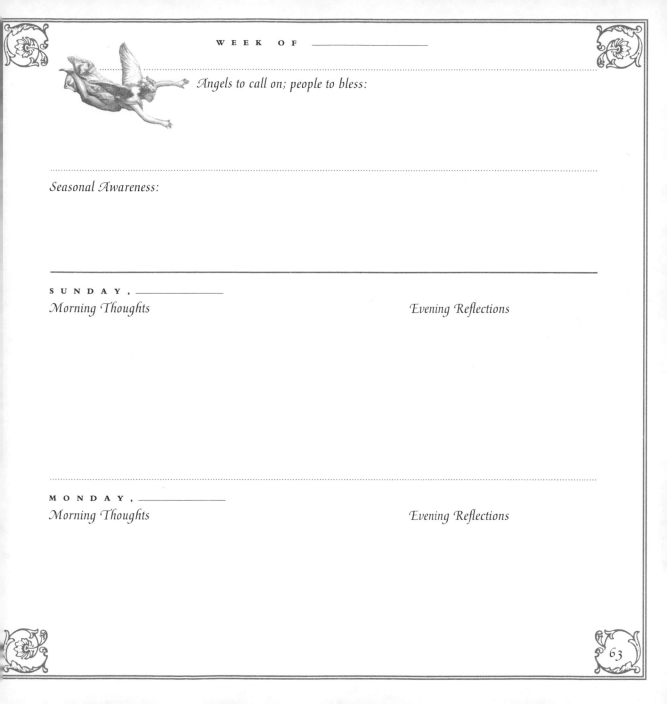

WEEK OF _____

Angels to call on; people to bless:

Seasonal Awareness:

SUNDAY, _____
Morning Thoughts   *Evening Reflections*

MONDAY, _____
Morning Thoughts   *Evening Reflections*

TUESDAY, _____
Morning Thoughts   *Evening Reflections*

WEDNESDAY, _____
Morning Thoughts   *Evening Reflections*

THURSDAY, _____
Morning Thoughts   *Evening Reflections*

FRIDAY, _____

Morning Thoughts   *Evening Reflections*

SATURDAY, _____

Morning Thoughts   *Evening Reflections*

Thoughts About the Week:

Education

Life is our school. Through living we find our own special way of becoming a Divine being and sharing our special ray of light with the world. The angels teach us about our hearts, our hearts teach us who we are.

CONTEMPLATION

The angels of light bring the air alive
Reminding me the time of inner growth is
at hand.
The Divine University of Life is in session
Offering me mindful illumination.
I am blessed with angelic tutelage as I venture into
The vast realms of spiritual knowledge and wisdom.

Goals:

Prayer requests
or notes to your
highest angel:

Concerns, worries,
fears to overcome:

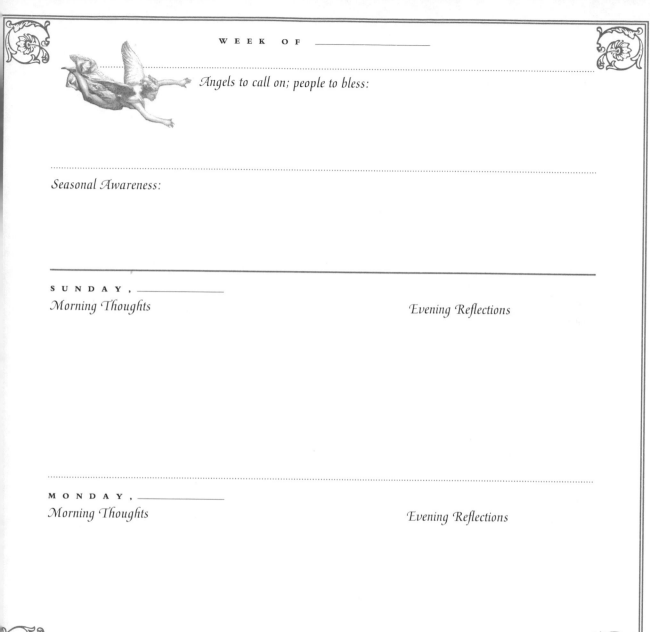

WEEK OF _____

Angels to call on; people to bless:

Seasonal Awareness:

SUNDAY, _____
Morning Thoughts   *Evening Reflections*

MONDAY, _____
Morning Thoughts   *Evening Reflections*

TUESDAY, _____

Morning Thoughts   *Evening Reflections*

WEDNESDAY, _____

Morning Thoughts   *Evening Reflections*

THURSDAY, _____

Morning Thoughts   *Evening Reflections*

WEEK OF _____

FRIDAY, _____

Morning Thoughts   *Evening Reflections*

SATURDAY, _____

Morning Thoughts   *Evening Reflections*

Thoughts About the Week:

Prosperity

P rosperity is the condition of being successful and prosperous. Prosperity is about flourishing and thriving. Thriving is about living and enjoying life. You are living in a new world of wealth with the angels in your consciousness. This world may have the same physical location, but your mind has taken on a new dimension of perception.

YOU ARE RICH IN ANGELS

- *Those things that make life meaningful are all around us in great quantity. By choosing to evolve and make things happen for ourselves, instead of depending on others and on the status quo for our prosperity, we become truly wealthy.*

- *Think about what you take with you at the end of your Earth life. You take your experiences, your memories, those times you took risks really to live. None of these intangibles has anything to do with money per se, but everything to do with thriving and truly living.*

Goals:

Prayer requests
or notes to your
highest angel:

Concerns, worries,
fears to overcome:

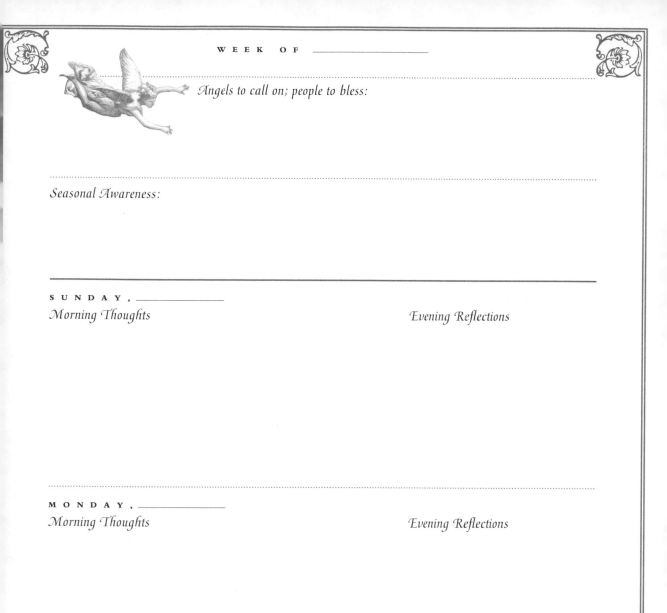

Angels to call on; people to bless:

Seasonal Awareness:

SUNDAY, _____

Morning Thoughts   *Evening Reflections*

MONDAY, _____

Morning Thoughts   *Evening Reflections*

T U E S D A Y , _____

Morning Thoughts

Evening Reflections

W E D N E S D A Y , _____

Morning Thoughts

Evening Reflections

T H U R S D A Y , _____

Morning Thoughts

Evening Reflections

WEEK OF _____

FRIDAY, _____

Morning Thoughts   *Evening Reflections*

SATURDAY, _____

Morning Thoughts   *Evening Reflections*

Thoughts About the Week:

73

ANGELIC SPIRIT OF THE WEEK

Providence

We are under Divine care and guardianship. For some that knowledge is enough, for others it calls forth a rebellion. At the moment we allow ourselves to be comfortable with who we came here to be, a signal goes out to Providence to help us know the way with abundant gifts and surprises.

CONTEMPLATION

Help comes from angels in unseen places and provides visible effects.
I open to Providence knowing there is no other way to discover my power.
My heart is humbled by generous help along the way,
the angels are guiding me.
The dream opens up to unlimited possibilities and angels.
I have joined Providence.

Goals:

Prayer requests
or notes to your
highest angel:

Concerns, worries,
fears to overcome:

WEEK OF _____

Angels to call on; people to bless:

Seasonal Awareness:

SUNDAY, _____
Morning Thoughts   *Evening Reflections*

MONDAY, _____
Morning Thoughts   *Evening Reflections*

TUESDAY, _____

Morning Thoughts

Evening Reflections

WEDNESDAY, _____

Morning Thoughts

Evening Reflections

THURSDAY, _____

Morning Thoughts

Evening Reflections

FRIDAY, _____

Morning Thoughts   *Evening Reflections*

SATURDAY, _____

Morning Thoughts   *Evening Reflections*

Thoughts About the Week:

Simplicity

S implicity is a Holy state, one of true humility, no pretensions, and *pure* intelligence. If you have a problem with simplicity, look for the core reason. Sometimes we overlook something or disregard it because it is just too simple to do. What a mistake that can be! Simplicity is honorable and we can bring it to all aspects of our lives. Human needs are basically very simple, and it is best to keep them this way when you want really to enjoy life and live creatively.

KEEP IT SIMPLE

- *Think about ways you can simplify your life in order to bring home more enjoyment and more contact with the angels. Let go of things that you don't really need, if they consume valuable time. Look for things to gather if they help you organize and save time.*
- *Pay attention to what is obvious!*

Goals:

Prayer requests
or notes to your
highest angel:

Concerns, worries,
fears to overcome:

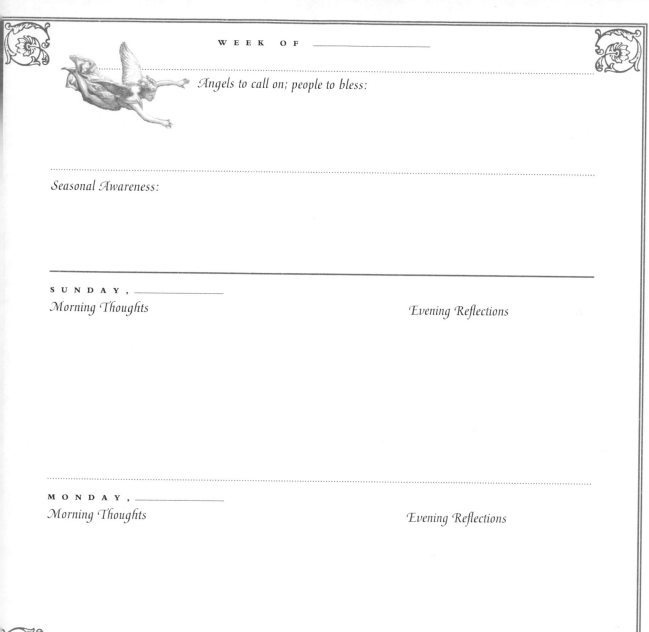

WEEK OF _____

Angels to call on; people to bless:

Seasonal Awareness:

SUNDAY, _____

Morning Thoughts   *Evening Reflections*

MONDAY, _____

Morning Thoughts   *Evening Reflections*

TUESDAY, ——————————

Morning Thoughts   *Evening Reflections*

WEDNESDAY, ——————————

Morning Thoughts   *Evening Reflections*

THURSDAY, ——————————

Morning Thoughts   *Evening Reflections*

FRIDAY, _____

Morning Thoughts

Evening Reflections

SATURDAY, _____

Morning Thoughts

Evening Reflections

Thoughts About the Week:

Devotion

D evotion means great love. When you devote yourself to something, you have vowed to follow it with love. Devotion does not mean becoming overly serious toward something. The angels teach us to devote ourselves to the light.

CONTEMPLATION

Without devotion I feel lost.
Without passion my senses are dull.
I will explore my Divine creative energy
and I will devote my heart and soul to it.
The angels are devoted to God's will.
I will be like the angels.

Goals:

Prayer requests
or notes to your
highest angel:

Concerns, worries,
fears to overcome:

WEEK OF _____

 Angels to call on; people to bless:

Seasonal Awareness:

_____

SUNDAY, _____
Morning Thoughts   *Evening Reflections*

....

MONDAY, _____
Morning Thoughts   *Evening Reflections*

WEEK OF _____

TUESDAY, _____
Morning Thoughts   *Evening Reflections*

WEDNESDAY, _____
Morning Thoughts   *Evening Reflections*

THURSDAY, _____
Morning Thoughts   *Evening Reflections*

FRIDAY, _____

Morning Thoughts   *Evening Reflections*

SATURDAY, _____

Morning Thoughts   *Evening Reflections*

Thoughts About the Week:

Vibrations

The angels are our creative partners in life. To allow their beneficial influence is a very simple concept: we must cultivate and develop qualities and attitudes to which the angels vibrate. For example, the vibration of greed is very low, and the angels vibrate only to very high notes. They can't help us if greed is ever a part of our intentions. On the other hand, beauty, prayer, gracious offerings, and simplicity, when practiced with a loving heart, bring us into creative harmony with the angels.

GOOD VIBRATIONS

- *To allow the angels to dance in our consciousness we must have a dance floor on which they can move. Basically, we raise our vibrations by being conscious of what we are doing and what effect we have on our environment.*
- *Our lives change when we bring the angels into our consciousness. Because the angels' vibrations are so high, the least little exchange with an angel lifts us beyond the petty mundane world and sets us on a path of magic and creativity. You will forever have an enlightened view once you sense the good vibrations of the angels.*

Goals:

Prayer requests
or notes to your
highest angel:

Concerns, worries,
fears to overcome:

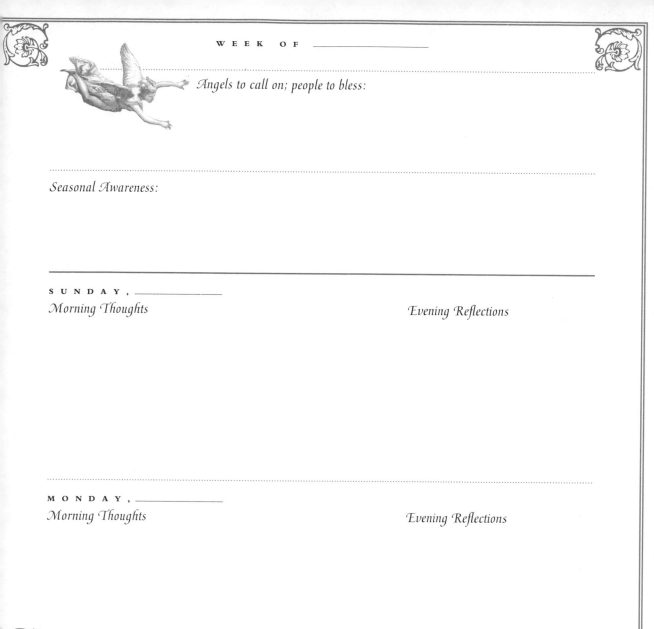

Angels to call on; people to bless:

Seasonal Awareness:

SUNDAY, _____

Morning Thoughts   _Evening Reflections_

MONDAY, _____

Morning Thoughts   _Evening Reflections_

TUESDAY, _____

Morning Thoughts   *Evening Reflections*

WEDNESDAY, _____

Morning Thoughts   *Evening Reflections*

THURSDAY, _____

Morning Thoughts   *Evening Reflections*

FRIDAY, _____
Morning Thoughts   *Evening Reflections*

SATURDAY, _____
Morning Thoughts   *Evening Reflections*

Thoughts About the Week:

ANGELIC SPIRIT OF THE WEEK

Wildness

*W*ildness means letting go. Accepting freedom. The greatest freedom comes when we set ourselves free of others' projections and expectations. This takes effort, but we have the angels to help us do it right. We have a wild life to live.

CONTEMPLATION

My way to freedom is revealed, wildness has set me in motion.
Wildness is a determined spirit compelling me to let go of convention.
Sparks ignite a fire in my soul. I will allow it to burn but not
scorch my spirit.
There is a constant part of me left to the wild,
undomesticated, and untamed.
My own wildness is gentle and loving, I allow it to inspire and excite.
I will dance in the light of the moon, and honor the sun by day.

Goals:

Prayer requests
or notes to your
highest angel:

Concerns, worries,
fears to overcome:

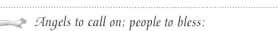

Angels to call on; people to bless:

Seasonal Awareness:

S U N D A Y , _____

Morning Thoughts   *Evening Reflections*

....

M O N D A Y , _____

Morning Thoughts   *Evening Reflections*

TUESDAY , _____
Morning Thoughts   *Evening Reflections*

WEDNESDAY , _____
Morning Thoughts   *Evening Reflections*

THURSDAY , _____
Morning Thoughts   *Evening Reflections*

FRIDAY, _____

Morning Thoughts   *Evening Reflections*

SATURDAY, _____

Morning Thoughts   *Evening Reflections*

Thoughts About the Week:

ANGELIC SPIRIT OF THE WEEK

Ground

*H*aving a human experience means we are in "ground school." The Earth is our true way to enlightenment. When we find beauty in the ordinary, it becomes extraordinary. The angels teach us to find beauty and worth in all our earthly activities. It is paradoxical that the angels, who spend their time in a realm other than the Earth, exist to teach us to be more human and more involved in our earthly experience as a way to know the Divine.

SOMETHING TO THINK ABOUT

- *Being in the physical realm in a human body is the only time we can physically touch our loved ones or create physical ways to transmit our special brand of love to the world.*

- *Grounding ourselves means that we touch and connect with the Earth. We are electrical beings and electricity needs to be grounded in order to be useful.*

Goals:

*Prayer requests
or notes to your
highest angel:*

*Concerns, worries,
fears to overcome:*

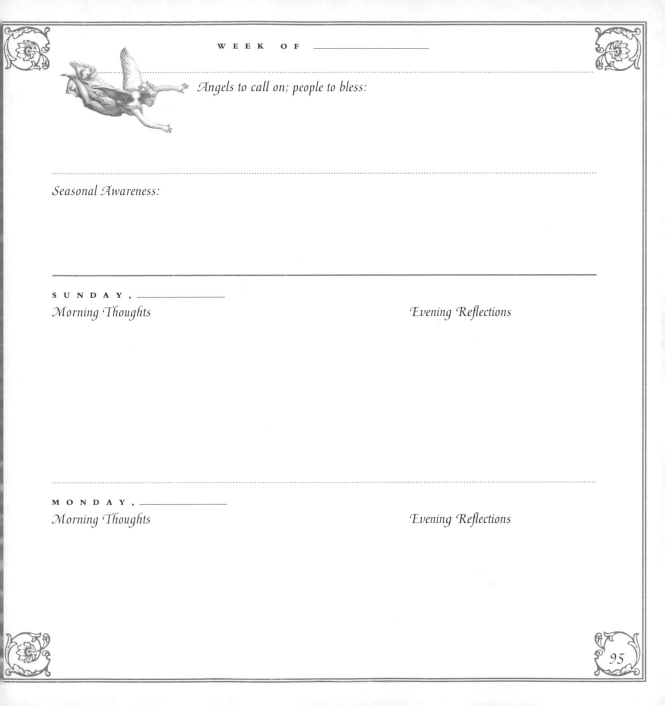

Angels to call on; people to bless:

Seasonal Awareness:

SUNDAY, _____
Morning Thoughts   *Evening Reflections*

MONDAY, _____
Morning Thoughts   *Evening Reflections*

TUESDAY, _____

Morning Thoughts   *Evening Reflections*

WEDNESDAY, _____

Morning Thoughts   *Evening Reflections*

THURSDAY, _____

Morning Thoughts   *Evening Reflections*

FRIDAY, _____

Morning Thoughts   *Evening Reflections*

SATURDAY, _____

Morning Thoughts   *Evening Reflections*

Thoughts About the Week:

Adventure

*T*rue adventure does not depend on traveling far and wide, or meeting a stream of new and interesting people. The great adventure is your life, the person you came here to be. When you open up to what life offers in each moment and you heed the calls and messages, the adventure never ends.

CONTEMPLATION

I let go of my ideals and they become my life.
I open to life and all becomes real and significant.
The spirit of adventure calls to my soul and I am
willing to take risks to live now.
I know that when I am happy in my own backyard,
I will be happy wherever I go.
The angels go with me.

Goals:

Prayer requests
or notes to your
highest angel:

Concerns, worries,
fears to overcome:

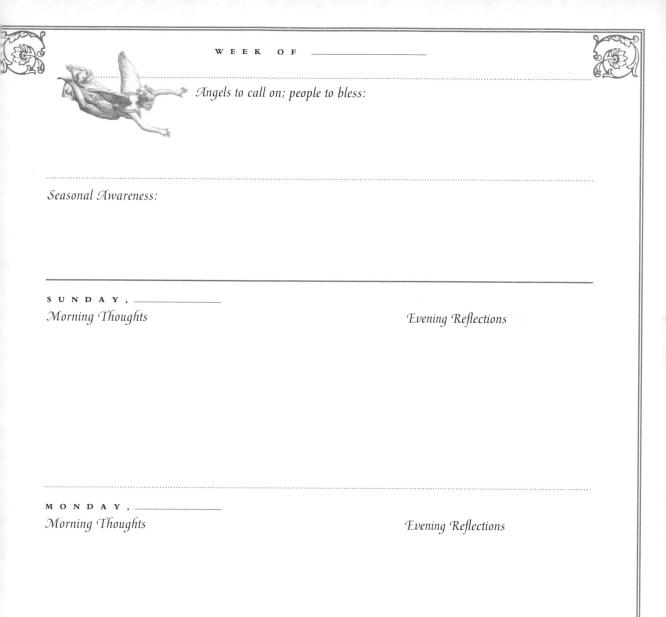

WEEK OF _____

....

Angels to call on; people to bless:

....

Seasonal Awareness:

_____

SUNDAY, _____

Morning Thoughts   *Evening Reflections*

....

MONDAY, _____

Morning Thoughts   *Evening Reflections*

TUESDAY, _____

Morning Thoughts   *Evening Reflections*

WEDNESDAY, _____

Morning Thoughts   *Evening Reflections*

THURSDAY, _____

Morning Thoughts   *Evening Reflections*

FRIDAY, ———————————

Morning Thoughts   *Evening Reflections*

SATURDAY, ———————————

Morning Thoughts   *Evening Reflections*

Thoughts About the Week:

Music

M usic is the cosmic dance, the sacred rhythm of the world's soul. Music can heal our lives by feeding the soul like vitamins feed the body. Music lifts our spirits and inspires our hearts to sing. Music is all around us, forever playing on in this vast Universe. There is music everywhere. Listen with your heart and you will know the angels.

LET LIFE BE MUSICAL

- *Collect different types of music to match your moods. Choose recordings that can serve as "soundtracks" for special moments in your life.*
- *Respond to music: dance, sing, play along, drum, move, delight, cry, laugh, make funny noises, or just sit quietly and go on a journey.*
- *Don't let a day go by without appreciating a moment of music.*

Goals:

*Prayer requests
or notes to your
highest angel:*

*Concerns, worries,
fears to overcome:*

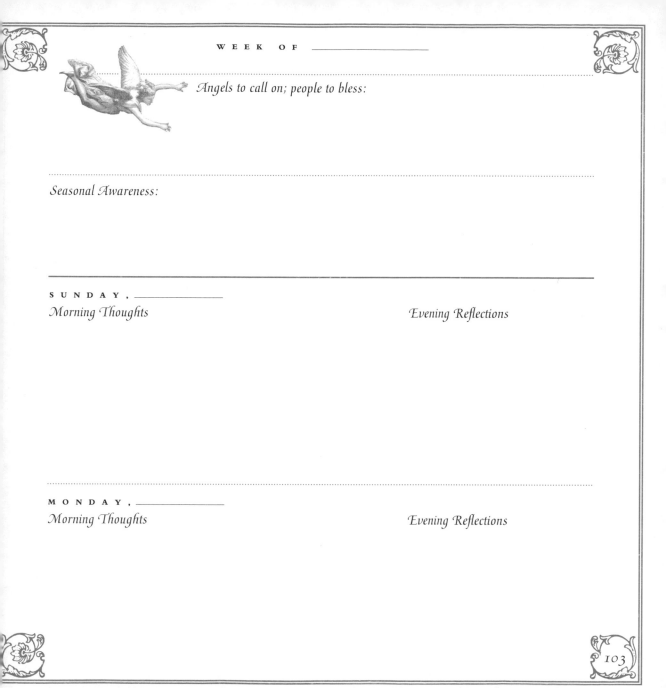

WEEK OF _____

Angels to call on; people to bless:

Seasonal Awareness:

SUNDAY, _____

Morning Thoughts   *Evening Reflections*

MONDAY, _____

Morning Thoughts   *Evening Reflections*

T U E S D A Y , _____

Morning Thoughts   *Evening Reflections*

W E D N E S D A Y , _____

Morning Thoughts   *Evening Reflections*

T H U R S D A Y , _____

Morning Thoughts   *Evening Reflections*

WEEK OF _____

FRIDAY, _____
Morning Thoughts   Evening Reflections

SATURDAY, _____
Morning Thoughts   Evening Reflections

Thoughts About the Week:

Humanness

A human birth is a miracle beyond comprehension. A human life becomes a gift to the world when life is respected, honored, and used for pure truth and beauty. When they allow themselves to be inspired by the angels, humans have the ability to create great art that will inspire the world for eons. The greatest asset in being human is that we may love deeply and truly.

CONTEMPLATION

I love being human.
I will be the best person that I can.
I am here to love.
I am here to share.
I am here to radiate light.
I am inspired to help Heaven.

Goals:

Prayer requests
or notes to your
highest angel:

Concerns, worries,
fears to overcome:

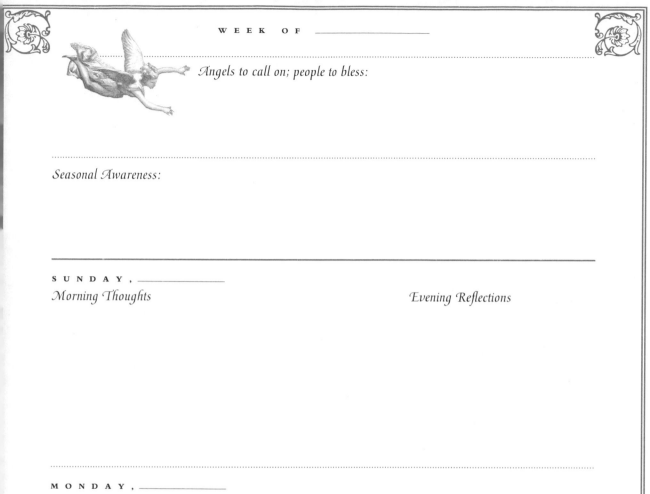

Angels to call on; people to bless:

Seasonal Awareness:

S U N D A Y , _____

Morning Thoughts   *Evening Reflections*

M O N D A Y , _____

Morning Thoughts   *Evening Reflections*

WEEK OF _____

TUESDAY, _____

Morning Thoughts   *Evening Reflections*

WEDNESDAY, _____

Morning Thoughts   *Evening Reflections*

THURSDAY, _____

Morning Thoughts   *Evening Reflections*

WEEK OF _____

....

FRIDAY , _____

Morning Thoughts   *Evening Reflections*

....

SATURDAY , _____

Morning Thoughts   *Evening Reflections*

Thoughts About the Week:

Levity

Levity means lightness of speech or attitude. It is the opposite of a heavy and despondent attitude. If we get stuck in a weighty attitude, we can always choose to bring some levity our way and the angels will love to help us. When in doubt, take it lightly as the angels do.

LIGHTEN UP

What is the absolute worst thing that can happen to us? When you find your answer, think beyond it and convince yourself that no matter what happens to us we are always loved and the love we have is always present; therefore, we will always be present and loved regardless of what form we take. Is there really any proof for the idea that life is serious?

Goals:

Prayer requests
or notes to your
highest angel:

Concerns, worries,
fears to overcome:

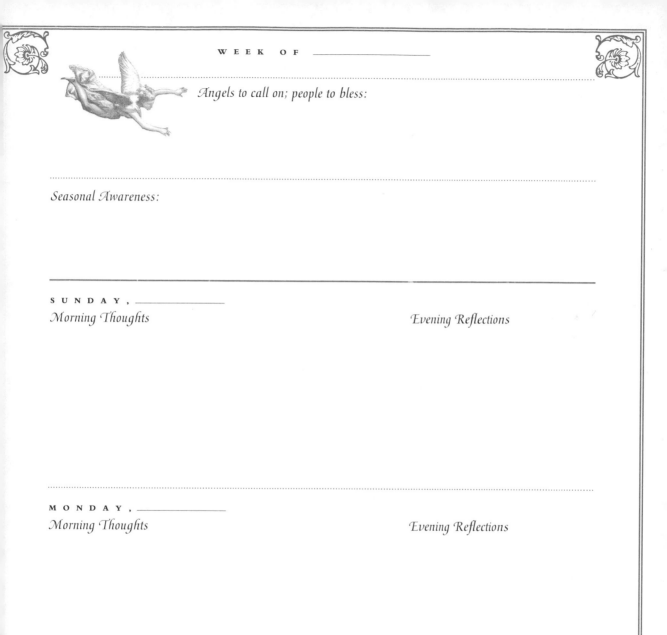

WEEK OF _____

Angels to call on; people to bless:

Seasonal Awareness:

SUNDAY, _____
Morning Thoughts   *Evening Reflections*

MONDAY, _____
Morning Thoughts   *Evening Reflections*

TUESDAY, _____

Morning Thoughts   *Evening Reflections*

WEDNESDAY, _____

Morning Thoughts   *Evening Reflections*

THURSDAY, _____

Morning Thoughts   *Evening Reflections*

F R I D A Y , _____

Morning Thoughts   *Evening Reflections*

S A T U R D A Y , _____

Morning Thoughts   *Evening Reflections*

Thoughts About the Week:

Relevance

Relevance has to do with the matter at hand, the immediate importance or significance of something. Its Latin origin is in the word *relevare*, to lift up. Sometimes we lift something to a level of importance that it simply doesn't deserve. It is important to stay awake to what is truly relevant in our lives. The angels are master teachers in this area.

THINKING STREAM

- *Although there is significance in many things, the most important picture is the* big picture.
- *Think of what is important to you and ask yourself if it is relevant to the big picture.*
- *Are your "feelings" really an indication of what is so important to you?*
- *What are feelings and where do they originate?*
- *Think about what you want to lift up in your life and what you would like to discard.*

Goals:

Prayer requests
or notes to your
highest angel:

Concerns, worries,
fears to overcome:

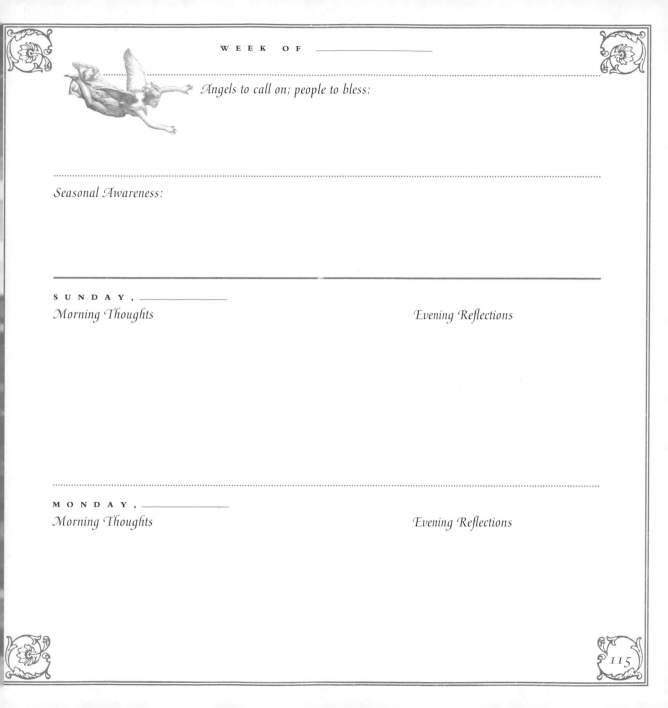

WEEK OF _____

Angels to call on; people to bless:

Seasonal Awareness:

SUNDAY, _____

Morning Thoughts   *Evening Reflections*

MONDAY, _____

Morning Thoughts   *Evening Reflections*

115

TUESDAY, _____

Morning Thoughts   *Evening Reflections*

WEDNESDAY, _____

Morning Thoughts   *Evening Reflections*

THURSDAY, _____

Morning Thoughts   *Evening Reflections*

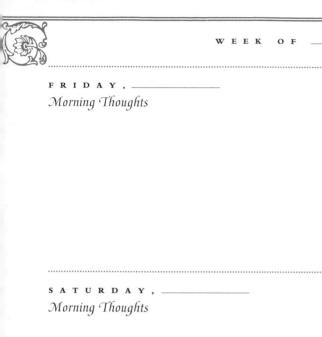

WEEK OF _____

FRIDAY, _____

Morning Thoughts   *Evening Reflections*

SATURDAY, _____

Morning Thoughts   *Evening Reflections*

Thoughts About the Week:

Consciousness

With consciousness, we are capable of a complex response to our environment. We are not sleepwalking, our actions are intentional and deliberate. When we are conscious of angels, we experience them on as many levels as we can possibly accept in the moment, and our awareness extends into thinking, feeling, and physical sensations without limiting our experiences. Once you are awake to something, it will keep you alert, you won't be able to shut your mind off to it completely. Therefore, it is important to be aware of your consciousness and your intent.

CONTEMPLATION

I am aware of myself and my existence.
I am awake to life rich with meaning and depth.
I see and know my reason for being.
Consciousness is love that expands and grows
with each loving thought I have for the Divine.
I will use my own angel consciousness to be of service to the Divine.

Goals:

Prayer requests
or notes to your
highest angel:

Concerns, worries,
fears to overcome:

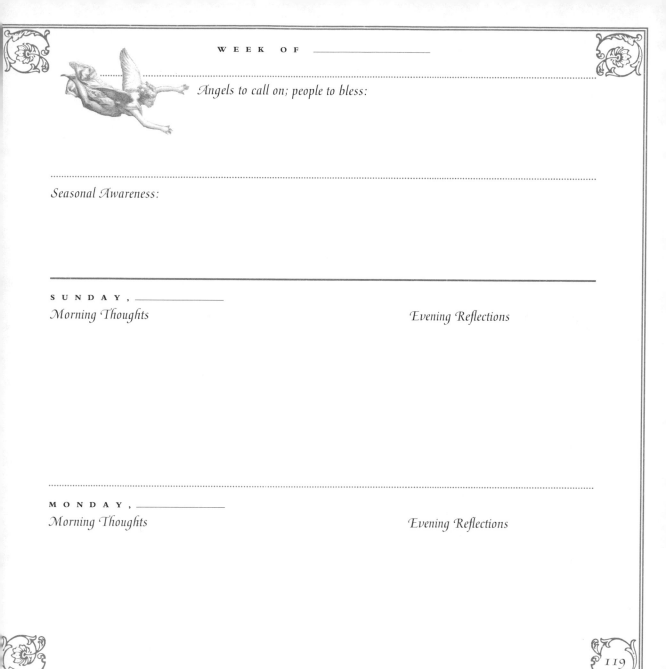

WEEK OF _____

Angels to call on; people to bless:

Seasonal Awareness:

SUNDAY, _____
Morning Thoughts   *Evening Reflections*

MONDAY, _____
Morning Thoughts   *Evening Reflections*

TUESDAY, _____

Morning Thoughts   *Evening Reflections*

WEDNESDAY, _____

Morning Thoughts   *Evening Reflections*

THURSDAY, _____

Morning Thoughts   *Evening Reflections*

....

FRIDAY, _____

Morning Thoughts   *Evening Reflections*

....

SATURDAY, _____

Morning Thoughts   *Evening Reflections*

_____

Thoughts About the Week:

ANGELIC SPIRIT OF THE WEEK

Learning

Do you need a teacher in order to learn something? Are all teachers human? Some of the best teachers are nonhuman—a tree, a flower, the sky, a seed, a kitten, a butterfly, an angel. When you learn something, it does not necessarily mean the lesson is over. It may have just begun. Sometimes it is proper to unlearn something.

THESE WORDS INDICATE LEARNING

mastery

accumulating knowledge

comprehend

experience, explore, experiment

study

watch, notice, examine

listen

Question!

....

Goals:

....

Prayer requests
or notes to your
highest angel:

....

Concerns, worries,
fears to overcome:

WEEK OF _____

....

Angels to call on; people to bless:

....

Seasonal Awareness:

_____

SUNDAY, _____

Morning Thoughts   *Evening Reflections*

....

MONDAY, _____

Morning Thoughts   *Evening Reflections*

123

TUESDAY, _____

Morning Thoughts

Evening Reflections

WEDNESDAY, _____

Morning Thoughts

Evening Reflections

THURSDAY, _____

Morning Thoughts

Evening Reflections

WEEK OF _____

FRIDAY, _____

Morning Thoughts

Evening Reflections

SATURDAY, _____

Morning Thoughts

Evening Reflections

Thoughts About the Week:

A N G E L I C   S P I R I T   O F   T H E   W E E K

Humor

Humor is our life preserver in the seas of uncertainty. Sometimes humor seems so out of reach that we worry we will drown before we can grasp it. But there is always humor in the heart of the moment. In a moment of panic, if we remove ourselves from the fear of the future and the terror of the past, we will see that humor is always there in full color. Our task is to reach for it, and laugh with the angels.

C O N T E M P L A T I O N

I welcome humor to lighten the dark.
I cherish it in my relationships.
The angels know humor is good for my soul;
they feed me with laughter when I need it the most.
When I stop to recognize laughter I feel a smile beginning to radiate
throughout my entire being.
I shall bask in Divine humor.

Goals:

Prayer requests
or notes to your
highest angel:

Concerns, worries,
fears to overcome:

Angels to call on; people to bless:

Seasonal Awareness:

SUNDAY, _____

Morning Thoughts   *Evening Reflections*

MONDAY, _____

Morning Thoughts   *Evening Reflections*

TUESDAY, _____

Morning Thoughts   *Evening Reflections*

WEDNESDAY, _____

Morning Thoughts   *Evening Reflections*

THURSDAY, _____

Morning Thoughts   *Evening Reflections*

FRIDAY, _____
Morning Thoughts   *Evening Reflections*

SATURDAY, _____
Morning Thoughts   *Evening Reflections*

Thoughts About the Week:

ANGELIC SPIRIT OF THE WEEK

Recognition

W hen we recognize something, we understand it again. To recognize something in someone else means that we possess that something too. This can be for better or for worse, depending on how willing we are to accept all parts of ourselves. The good news is that when we recognize greatness in another we are doing it from that same place in ourselves. When you recognize the angels, you have come to know God in your own way.

SELF-RECOGNITION

- *What do I usually recognize or notice in others?*
- *What am I recognized for?*
- *Do I crave recognition?*
- *Do I limit what I recognize with unconscious negativity?*
- *How may I recognize the angels in my life?*

Goals:

*Prayer requests
or notes to your
highest angel:*

*Concerns, worries,
fears to overcome:*

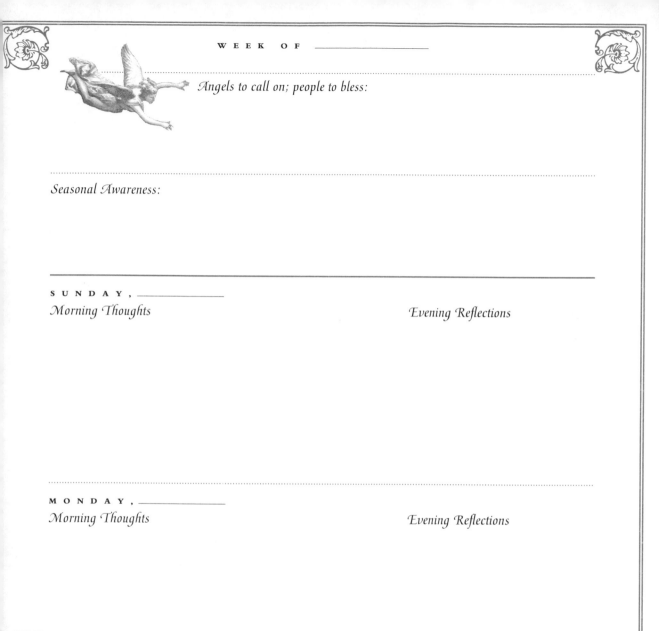

WEEK OF _____

Angels to call on; people to bless:

Seasonal Awareness:

SUNDAY, _____
Morning Thoughts   *Evening Reflections*

MONDAY, _____
Morning Thoughts   *Evening Reflections*

TUESDAY, _____

Morning Thoughts   *Evening Reflections*

WEDNESDAY, _____

Morning Thoughts   *Evening Reflections*

THURSDAY, _____

Morning Thoughts   *Evening Reflections*

FRIDAY, _____

Morning Thoughts   *Evening Reflections*

SATURDAY, _____

Morning Thoughts   *Evening Reflections*

Thoughts About the Week:

Breath

*W*e breathe, which verifies that we are alive. When we say we need to "take a breather," we want to rest and take stock of what is happening around us. *Inspire* means breath taken in, *aspire* means to breathe upon, to desire. Allow yourself a good breather often. It will help keep things in heavenly perspective. The angels aspire to inspire humans. God is breathing on us.

CONTEMPLATION

Deep peace is in the air around me.
I breathe peace into the corners of my consciousness.
Breath keeps me alive, the angels are God's breath upon me.
Breath of God, fill me with Divine inspiration so that my life will be a peaceful statement of love.

Goals:

Prayer requests
or notes to your
highest angel:

Concerns, worries,
fears to overcome:

WEEK OF _____

Angels to call on; people to bless:

Seasonal Awareness:

SUNDAY, _____

Morning Thoughts   *Evening Reflections*

MONDAY, _____

Morning Thoughts   *Evening Reflections*

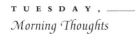

T U E S D A Y , _____

Morning Thoughts   *Evening Reflections*

W E D N E S D A Y , _____

Morning Thoughts   *Evening Reflections*

T H U R S D A Y , _____

Morning Thoughts   *Evening Reflections*

FRIDAY, _____
Morning Thoughts   *Evening Reflections*

SATURDAY, _____
Morning Thoughts   *Evening Reflections*

Thoughts About the Week:

ANGELIC SPIRIT OF THE WEEK

Thought

*T*hinking is a process of: calling something to our minds, imagining, remembering, pondering, reasoning, inventing, visualizing, exploring, shedding light on a subject, questioning, contemplating, tracking, and playing. It is important to think and not to limit thoughts. We must spend enough time in thought so that limits vanish naturally. Our imagination is a place of truth. There is truth in fantasy, and fantasy in truth.

THINK ON THESE THINGS

- *What is freedom?*
- *What is bad? (Think through each thing you come up with and find something "not bad" about it.)*
- *What does "meant to be" mean to you?*
- *What is really serious about life?*
- *What are your innermost values, those which you would consider fighting to defend?*

Goals:

Prayer requests
or notes to your
highest angel:

Concerns, worries,
fears to overcome:

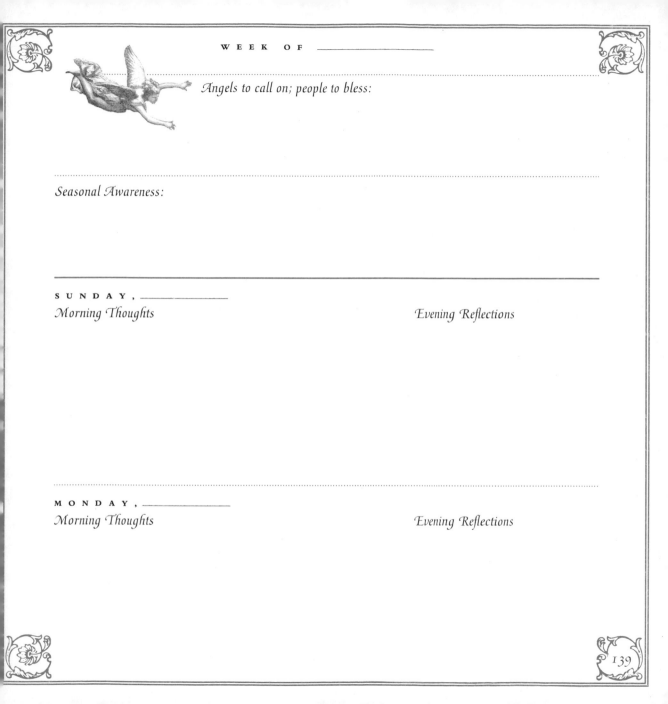

WEEK OF _____

Angels to call on; people to bless:

Seasonal Awareness:

SUNDAY, _____

Morning Thoughts   *Evening Reflections*

MONDAY, _____

Morning Thoughts   *Evening Reflections*

139

TUESDAY, ———————————

Morning Thoughts   *Evening Reflections*

WEDNESDAY, ———————————

Morning Thoughts   *Evening Reflections*

THURSDAY, ———————————

Morning Thoughts   *Evening Reflections*

FRIDAY, _____

Morning Thoughts   *Evening Reflections*

SATURDAY, _____

Morning Thoughts   *Evening Reflections*

Thoughts About the Week:

Trust

We have been entrusted with a special gift, life. God has trusted us with many blessings and it is important that we respond to our blessings with the utmost care, concern, and gratitude. For if we neglect or misuse our Divine gifts, the Universe will no longer trust in us and give abundantly. Think of what you have going in your life: are you doing the best you can? Have you truly allowed the angels to inspire your greatness? It is more important to do a few things well and completely than to do many things halfway and without spirit.

CONTEMPLATION

I will not worry over those things with which I have been entrusted,
for worry is the opposite of trust.
I will enjoy my responsibilities and bring love to them.
The more I do things with love and service in my heart,
the more bounty I will be entrusted with.
God gives to those who are able to receive love.

Goals:

Prayer requests
or notes to your
highest angel:

Concerns, worries,
fears to overcome:

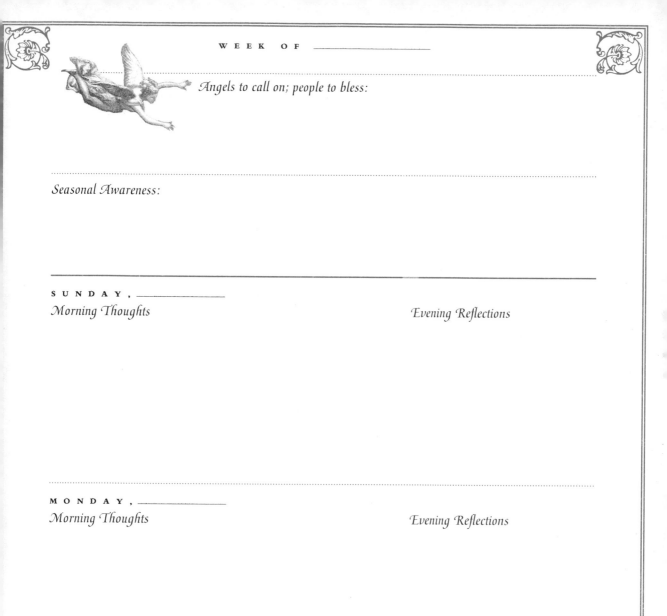

WEEK OF _____

Angels to call on; people to bless:

Seasonal Awareness:

SUNDAY, _____

Morning Thoughts   *Evening Reflections*

MONDAY, _____

Morning Thoughts   *Evening Reflections*

TUESDAY, _____
Morning Thoughts   *Evening Reflections*

WEDNESDAY, _____
Morning Thoughts   *Evening Reflections*

THURSDAY, _____
Morning Thoughts   *Evening Reflections*

FRIDAY, _____

Morning Thoughts   *Evening Reflections*

SATURDAY, _____

Morning Thoughts   *Evening Reflections*

Thoughts About the Week:

Messages

T he angels are Divine messengers of light who offer us guidance. How do we know when a message has been sent from the angels? Are we naturally in the right place at the right time? Our *willingness* to receive Divine guidance is what positions us at the right time and place for a message. If we make ourselves available to live in accordance with the Divine, then we will know in our hearts when an angelic message has been sent.

PLAY

- *Close your eyes right now and find a message that is waiting to come through.*
- *What does it mean—is it for you personally or is it of a global nature?*
- *If your life is a message, what is it saying?*
- *How can you filter out what is not part of an important message?*
- *What aspects of life can serve as messages (e.g., illness, opportunity, relationship)?*

Goals:

*Prayer requests
or notes to your
highest angel:*

*Concerns, worries,
fears to overcome:*

WEEK OF _____

....

Angels to call on; people to bless:

....

Seasonal Awareness:

_____

S U N D A Y , _____

Morning Thoughts   *Evening Reflections*

....

M O N D A Y , _____

Morning Thoughts   *Evening Reflections*

TUESDAY, _____

Morning Thoughts   *Evening Reflections*

WEDNESDAY, _____

Morning Thoughts   *Evening Reflections*

THURSDAY, _____

Morning Thoughts   *Evening Reflections*

FRIDAY, _____

Morning Thoughts   *Evening Reflections*

SATURDAY, _____

Morning Thoughts   *Evening Reflections*

Thoughts About the Week:

Caring

Basic human kindness and caring is the healing balm for our souls. When we feel that we are cared for, we have the strength to go out in the world with joy and peace. Even if just one person truly cares and we know it, this is enough.

Whom do you care about? Take more time to listen to those you care for. This is important. Love is a behavior.

CONTEMPLATION

I am not afraid to care deeply for another human.
There may be pain in caring, but that pain is beautiful,
for it is proof that I have loved.
I ask the angels to help me be a positive force of love on Earth.
I will go where I am needed.
I will care unconditionally and truly, for the glory of God.

Goals:

Prayer requests
or notes to your
highest angel:

Concerns, worries,
fears to overcome:

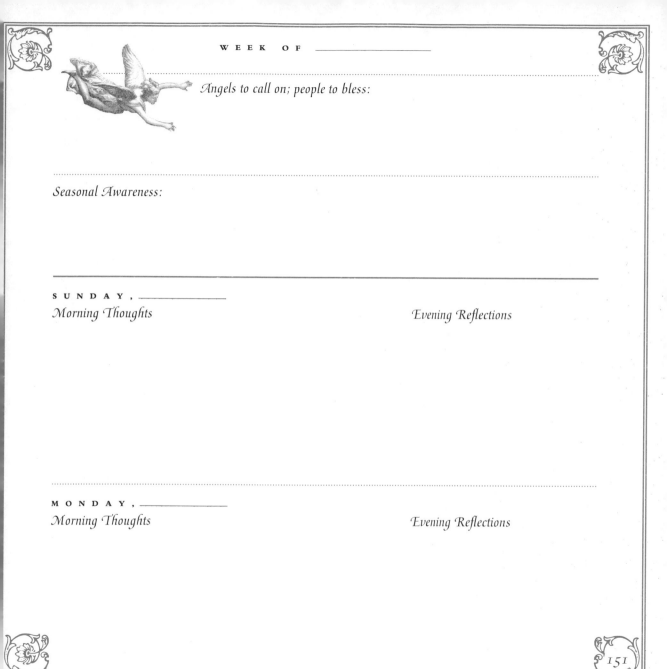

WEEK OF _____

Angels to call on; people to bless:

Seasonal Awareness:

SUNDAY, _____

Morning Thoughts   *Evening Reflections*

MONDAY, _____

Morning Thoughts   *Evening Reflections*

TUESDAY, _____

Morning Thoughts   *Evening Reflections*

WEDNESDAY, _____

Morning Thoughts   *Evening Reflections*

THURSDAY, _____

Morning Thoughts   *Evening Reflections*

FRIDAY, _____

Morning Thoughts   *Evening Reflections*

SATURDAY, _____

Morning Thoughts   *Evening Reflections*

Thoughts About the Week:

ANGELIC SPIRIT OF THE WEEK

Wonder

*W*hen we find wonder in something, we are in awe, marveling over a special surprise we happened upon. Wondering about something means that we are curious or in doubt about it. The angels are a wonder and they can make us ponder many things. Allow yourself to wander into wonder.

QUESTIONING STREAM

- *I wonder why . . . (finish):*
- *I find the following things wonder-full:*
- *To me, a miracle is:*
- *I have been awed by the following things in nature (e.g., hummingbirds, double rainbows, the aurora borealis—describe them on paper or in your mind):*

Goals:

Prayer requests or notes to your highest angel:

Concerns, worries, fears to overcome:

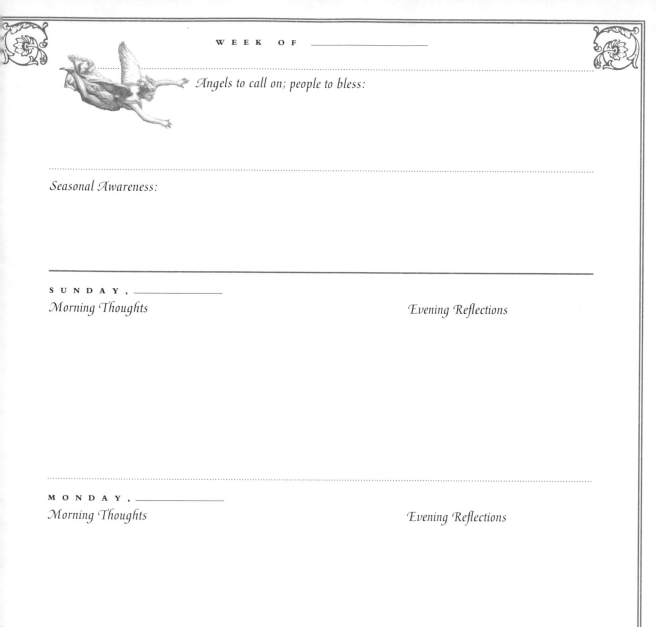

WEEK OF _____

Angels to call on; people to bless:

Seasonal Awareness:

SUNDAY, _____
Morning Thoughts   *Evening Reflections*

MONDAY, _____
Morning Thoughts   *Evening Reflections*

TUESDAY, _____

Morning Thoughts   *Evening Reflections*

WEDNESDAY, _____

Morning Thoughts   *Evening Reflections*

THURSDAY, _____

Morning Thoughts   *Evening Reflections*

FRIDAY, _____
Morning Thoughts   *Evening Reflections*

SATURDAY, _____
Morning Thoughts   *Evening Reflections*

Thoughts About the Week:

ANGELIC SPIRIT OF THE WEEK

Awareness

A wareness means being mindful, conscious, and cognizant, having true knowledge of what is happening on the inner and outer levels of your being. Knowing something means you are aware of it—you allow it to have many levels of discovery. Awareness is the most powerful tool humans possess, as far as spiritual, personal, and physical growth goes. Awareness of angels changes and expands your life.

CONTEMPLATION

Meaning is all around me, calling from the corners.
My heart hears the message that my eyes miss-take.
I will go back and start again, this time knowing that
a tree has many leaves, I move closer for a look.
I know that in the air I breathe live many beings of
light, many worlds that carry themselves on unseen frequencies.
My awareness defines who I am.

Goals:

Prayer requests
or notes to your
highest angel:

Concerns, worries,
fears to overcome:

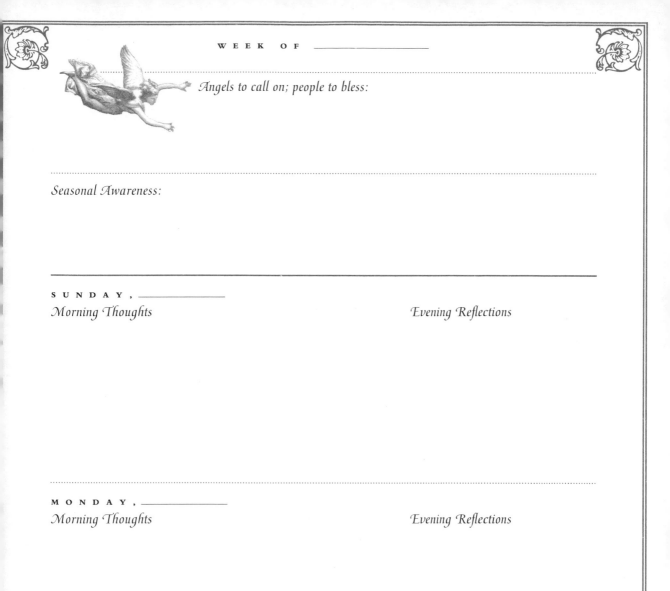

WEEK OF _____

Angels to call on; people to bless:

Seasonal Awareness:

SUNDAY, _____
Morning Thoughts   *Evening Reflections*

MONDAY, _____
Morning Thoughts   *Evening Reflections*

TUESDAY, ─────────────

Morning Thoughts   *Evening Reflections*

WEDNESDAY, ─────────────

Morning Thoughts   *Evening Reflections*

THURSDAY, ─────────────

Morning Thoughts   *Evening Reflections*

FRIDAY, _____

Morning Thoughts   *Evening Reflections*

SATURDAY, _____

Morning Thoughts   *Evening Reflections*

Thoughts About the Week:

Face

F ace is a word used for the front of things and for the act of turning to see the truth. A face is more important than we sometimes would like it to be. There is truth in a face. Faces radiate what is within us. The face of an angel is the face of God. With the angels in our consciousness our faces show love, understanding, and caring—the only way to radiate true beauty.

THINKING STREAM

- *Think about your own face, your own countenance.*
- *What truth have you had to face recently?*
- *Why would we face music?*
- *Can you smile with a stiff upper lip?*
- *Is your face always an honest map of who you are?*

Goals:

Prayer requests
or notes to your
highest angel:

Concerns, worries,
fears to overcome:

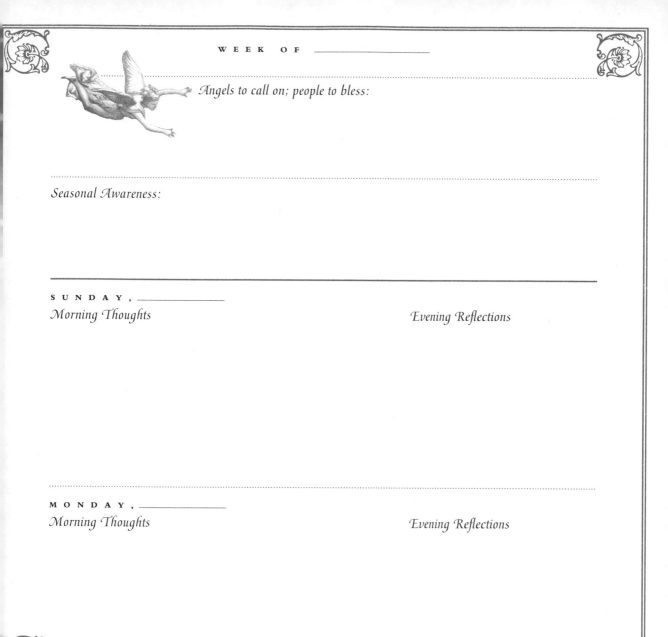

WEEK OF _____

Angels to call on; people to bless:

Seasonal Awareness:

SUNDAY, _____

Morning Thoughts   *Evening Reflections*

MONDAY, _____

Morning Thoughts   *Evening Reflections*

WEEK OF _____

TUESDAY, _____

Morning Thoughts   *Evening Reflections*

WEDNESDAY, _____

Morning Thoughts   *Evening Reflections*

THURSDAY, _____

Morning Thoughts   *Evening Reflections*

FRIDAY, _____

Morning Thoughts   *Evening Reflections*

SATURDAY, _____

Morning Thoughts   *Evening Reflections*

Thoughts About the Week:

Grace

D ivine grace cannot be bargained for or earned; it can only be accepted with a pure heart. Grace reminds us that we are forever held in the light of God's love. Grace and humility go hand in hand. When we feel that we cannot go on and we humble ourselves with surrender to God, the state of grace descends upon us like a beautiful golden blanket warming our hearts and souls with love.

CONTEMPLATION

God is love.

I cannot buy love or earn it.

It just is.

Just as the sun continues to shine on me no matter what I do,
God's love is always moving my heart gracefully through life
as the angels inspire my spirit upward.

Goals:

....

Prayer requests
or notes to your
highest angel:

....

Concerns, worries,
fears to overcome:

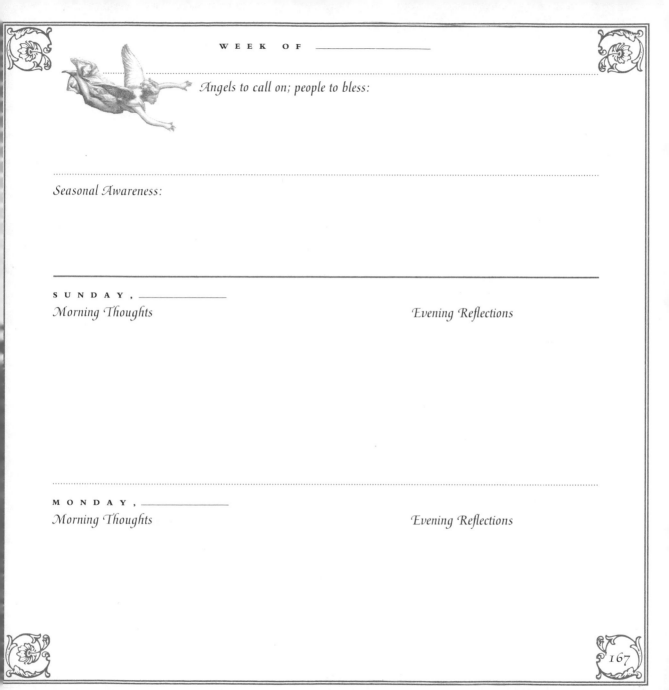

Angels to call on; people to bless:

Seasonal Awareness:

SUNDAY, _____

Morning Thoughts   *Evening Reflections*

MONDAY, _____

Morning Thoughts   *Evening Reflections*

TUESDAY, _____
Morning Thoughts   *Evening Reflections*

WEDNESDAY, _____
Morning Thoughts   *Evening Reflections*

THURSDAY, _____
Morning Thoughts   *Evening Reflections*

FRIDAY, _____

Morning Thoughts   *Evening Reflections*

SATURDAY, _____

Morning Thoughts   *Evening Reflections*

Thoughts About the Week:

ANGELIC SPIRIT OF THE WEEK

Resilience

T he word *resilient* comes from the Latin *resilire*, which means to leap back. When something is resilient it is elastic; it can go back to its original shape after being bent, stretched, and stressed. The more resilient our minds, the more quickly we can leap back to our natural state of inner peace after we are altered in a way that doesn't suit us. With the angels in our consciousness we are inherently more resilient.

STRESS TEST

- *Are you able to let petty grievances slide without a problem?*
- *Do you follow the "get back on the saddle" philosophy of life after meeting a setback?*
- *Do you welcome change without a lot of resistance?*
- *Is your mind open to new things?*
- *Is playing easy for you?*
- *Can you find peace in the moment?*
- *Do you understand the angels?*

Goals:

Prayer requests
or notes to your
highest angel:

Concerns, worries,
fears to overcome:

Angels to call on; people to bless:

Seasonal Awareness:

SUNDAY, _____
Morning Thoughts   *Evening Reflections*

MONDAY, _____
Morning Thoughts   *Evening Reflections*

TUESDAY, _____
Morning Thoughts   *Evening Reflections*

WEDNESDAY, _____
Morning Thoughts   *Evening Reflections*

THURSDAY, _____
Morning Thoughts   *Evening Reflections*

F R I D A Y , _____

Morning Thoughts   *Evening Reflections*

S A T U R D A Y , _____

Morning Thoughts   *Evening Reflections*

Thoughts About the Week:

Acceptance

A cceptance is the art of making peace with life, of leaving all our expectations and projected ideals at the door and entering a new world of truth and beauty. In the world of acceptance, we understand that without sorrow we will not know joy. The angels help us accept all of life. We allow ourselves to experience profound meaning and love.

C O N T E M P L A T I O N

Life offers what is perfect for me.
I accept my life with a heart of truth.
My journey through life is not my own,
my life belongs to the infinite wisdom of the Universe.
I am guided by loving beings who teach me about a peace
that surpasses all need for idealistic attachments or denial.
I accept.

Goals:

Prayer requests
or notes to your
highest angel:

Concerns, worries,
fears to overcome:

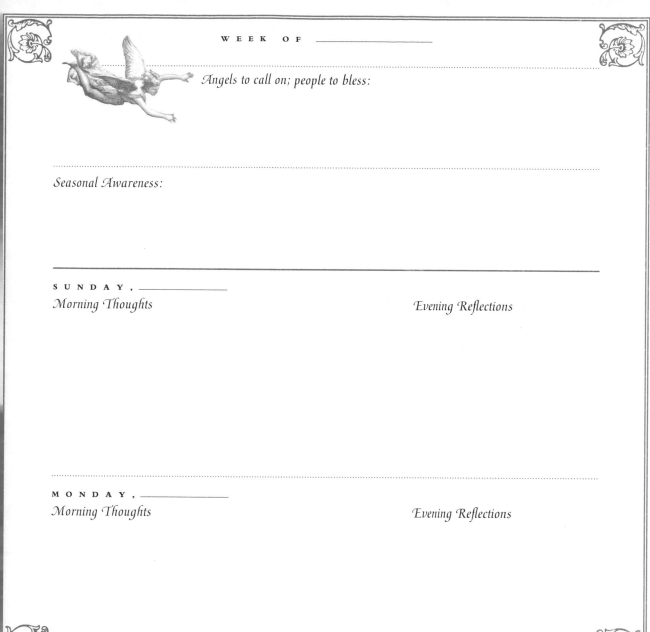

Angels to call on; people to bless:

Seasonal Awareness:

SUNDAY , _____
Morning Thoughts   *Evening Reflections*

MONDAY , _____
Morning Thoughts   *Evening Reflections*

WEEK OF ———————————

TUESDAY, ———————————

Morning Thoughts   *Evening Reflections*

WEDNESDAY, ———————————

Morning Thoughts   *Evening Reflections*

THURSDAY, ———————————

Morning Thoughts   *Evening Reflections*

FRIDAY, _____

Morning Thoughts   *Evening Reflections*

SATURDAY, _____

Morning Thoughts   *Evening Reflections*

Thoughts About the Week:

Nature

W ith the angels as our daily companions, nature takes on a new meaning. Flowers, trees, birds, and the clouds become our direct connection to the angels. The angels remind us to stop and "smell the roses" and to drink in the peace of the natural world each day.

IDEAS

- *Find a tree, bush, or flower and sketch it while you generate love for it.*
- *Ask Sister Moon a question and gaze at her until you have your answer.*
- *Listen to a bird singing and think about a message the angels may have for you.*
- *Understand how giving Brother Sun is.*
- *Find yourself a council of trees to advise you in decisions requiring strength.*
- *See the angels in the clouds and feel gratitude in your heart when you do.*

Goals:

Prayer requests
or notes to your
highest angel:

Concerns, worries,
fears to overcome:

Angels to call on; people to bless:

Seasonal Awareness:

SUNDAY, _____
Morning Thoughts   *Evening Reflections*

MONDAY, _____
Morning Thoughts   *Evening Reflections*

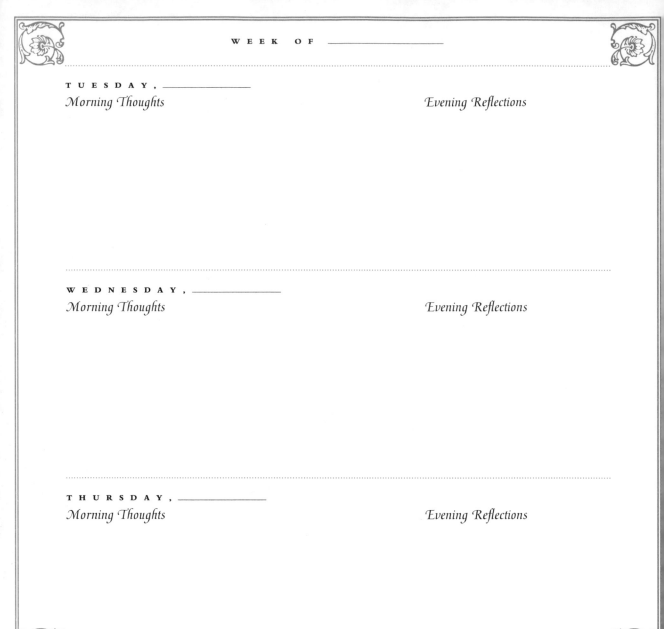

WEEK OF _____

TUESDAY, _____

Morning Thoughts   *Evening Reflections*

WEDNESDAY, _____

Morning Thoughts   *Evening Reflections*

THURSDAY, _____

Morning Thoughts   *Evening Reflections*

FRIDAY, _____

Morning Thoughts   *Evening Reflections*

SATURDAY, _____

Morning Thoughts   *Evening Reflections*

Thoughts About the Week:

Surrender

*S*urrender means to relinquish control. Surrender is odd in that it is our only true choice because we are not in control. If you think this is incorrect and that you are in control, think about what happens each night as you venture into dreamland—are you in control? When we surrender to the truth and beauty of the Universe, our lives will be given over to the greatest love available and the angels will maintain control.

CONTEMPLATION

I surrender to the loving guidance.
I give up to God, I go upwards and expand.
There is no need for control, there is no way to
tame my fears, for they do not exist in their worrisome form.
The fear of suffering is worse than actual suffering.
Illusion brings gloom.
I will surrender and give up illusion.

....

Goals:

....

Prayer requests
or notes to your
highest angel:

....

Concerns, worries,
fears to overcome:

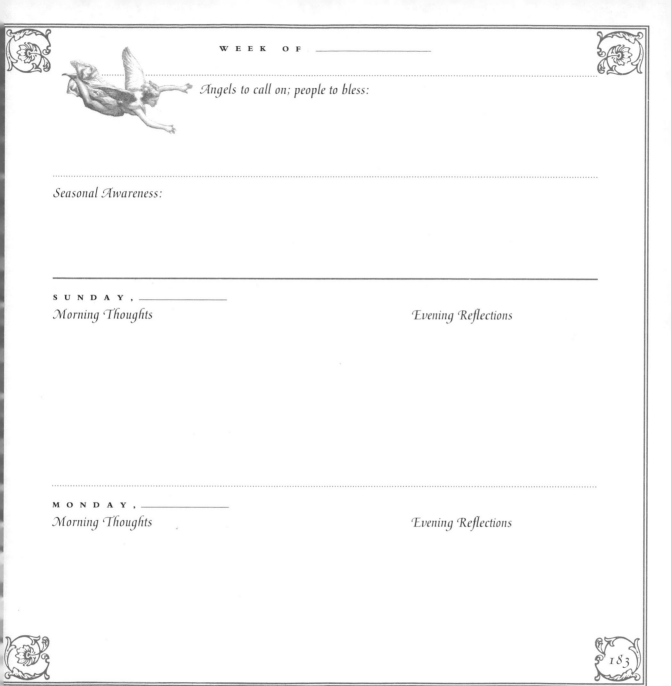

Angels to call on; people to bless:

Seasonal Awareness:

SUNDAY, _____

Morning Thoughts   *Evening Reflections*

MONDAY, _____

Morning Thoughts   *Evening Reflections*

TUESDAY, _____

Morning Thoughts

Evening Reflections

WEDNESDAY, _____

Morning Thoughts

Evening Reflections

THURSDAY, _____

Morning Thoughts

Evening Reflections

FRIDAY, _____
Morning Thoughts   *Evening Reflections*

SATURDAY, _____
Morning Thoughts   *Evening Reflections*

Thoughts About the Week:

ANGELIC SPIRIT OF THE WEEK

Climbing

Climbing is something we must do when we are ascending to new heights. Life on the spiritual path is a climb up a beautiful mountain, abundant with trees, rocks, and here and there an unexpected precipice to pass gingerly. If we focus on the climb itself, we may forget to be grateful for the beauty of the experience. The angels want us to remember the summit, the big picture, and not trip on the rocks or get caught in the branches during our sacred climb.

QUEST

- *Do you know where you are going, what you are climbing toward?*
- *Take a hike up a mountain, take your time and appreciate every step.*
- *Think about how natural it is for the angels to help us on our climb up the mountain of life.*
- *Think about the things we climb, such as a ladder, a mountain, stairs; and think about how climbing up gives you a different view and perspective on a situation.*

Goals:

Prayer requests or notes to your highest angel:

Concerns, worries, fears to overcome:

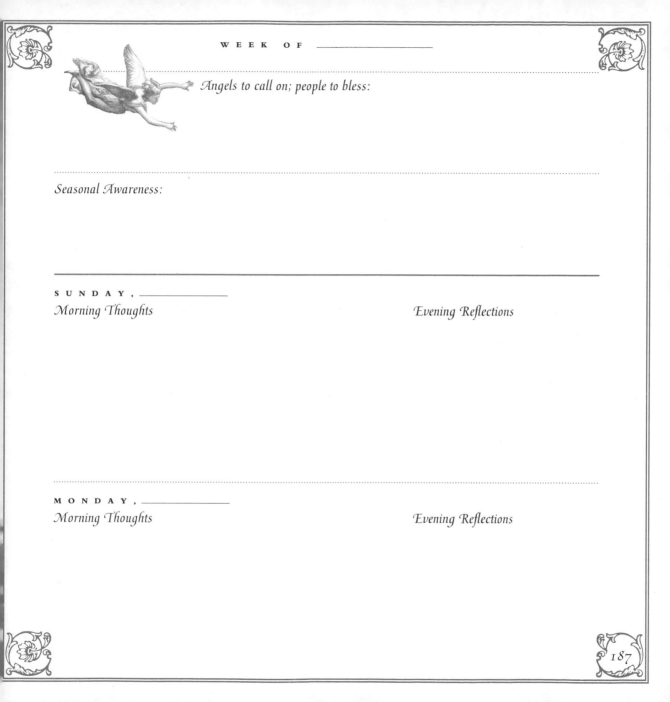

WEEK OF _____

Angels to call on; people to bless:

Seasonal Awareness:

SUNDAY, _____
Morning Thoughts   *Evening Reflections*

MONDAY, _____
Morning Thoughts   *Evening Reflections*

TUESDAY, _____
Morning Thoughts   *Evening Reflections*

WEDNESDAY, _____
Morning Thoughts   *Evening Reflections*

THURSDAY, _____
Morning Thoughts   *Evening Reflections*

FRIDAY, _____

Morning Thoughts   *Evening Reflections*

SATURDAY, _____

Morning Thoughts   *Evening Reflections*

Thoughts About the Week:

A N G E L I C   S P I R I T   O F   T H E   W E E K

Possibility

With God all things are possible. Why then do we attempt to limit the possible with our definitions and labels? We think there is a limit to what we can know, yet the world is unknowable because it is in process and full of endless possibilities. There are infinite angels waiting to help us discover the possible us.

I D E A S

- *To understand fully that all things are possible and that the supernatural is actually very normal and natural, you must explore the realm of your imagination and know that what happens in your imagination is limitless and very real.*
- *If the possible makes you uncomfortable, live with that discomfort. Don't try to make major shifts in your consciousness overnight. Live with your questions and quests and explore the wide range of possibilities life has to offer.*

Goals:

*Prayer requests
or notes to your
highest angel:*

*Concerns, worries,
fears to overcome:*

WEEK OF _____

Angels to call on; people to bless:

Seasonal Awareness:

SUNDAY, _____

Morning Thoughts   *Evening Reflections*

MONDAY, _____

Morning Thoughts   *Evening Reflections*

WEEK OF _____

TUESDAY, _____

Morning Thoughts   *Evening Reflections*

WEDNESDAY, _____

Morning Thoughts   *Evening Reflections*

THURSDAY, _____

Morning Thoughts   *Evening Reflections*

FRIDAY, _____

Morning Thoughts   *Evening Reflections*

SATURDAY, _____

Morning Thoughts   *Evening Reflections*

Thoughts About the Week:

ANGELIC SPIRIT OF THE WEEK

Synchronism

The universal heartbeat keeps its own pace. It is up to us to synchronize our own life-beat with the universal flow of energy. When we are in synch with the heavens, we are operating in unison with the angels. When we are in agreement with time, our lives are full of grace in the present.

S Y N C H R O N I C I T Y

- *How do you feel right now? If you are at peace, you are at one with the heart of the world.*

- *A synchronism is a coincidence in which you pay attention to the "something more" that is present as a message.*

- *It is no mere coincidence that you were born when you were, as who you are.*

....

Goals:

....

Prayer requests
or notes to your
highest angel:

....

Concerns, worries,
fears to overcome:

WEEK OF _____

Angels to call on; people to bless:

Seasonal Awareness:

SUNDAY, _____

Morning Thoughts   *Evening Reflections*

MONDAY, _____

Morning Thoughts   *Evening Reflections*

TUESDAY, _____
Morning Thoughts   *Evening Reflections*

WEDNESDAY, _____
Morning Thoughts   *Evening Reflections*

THURSDAY, _____
Morning Thoughts   *Evening Reflections*

FRIDAY, _____

Morning Thoughts   *Evening Reflections*

SATURDAY, _____

Morning Thoughts   *Evening Reflections*

Thoughts About the Week:

Calmness

C almness is a state of mind undisturbed by the rattle of emotions and the crash of worries. Calmness opens into tranquillity supreme. Serenity is ours when we allow the angels to quiet the turbulent forces of life and leave our souls in deep peace and stillness.

CONTEMPLATION

I am calm.

I am peaceful.

I know serenity.

My soul is bathed in tranquillity.

Nothing can disturb me.

God is within.

Goals:

Prayer requests
or notes to your
highest angel:

Concerns, worries,
fears to overcome:

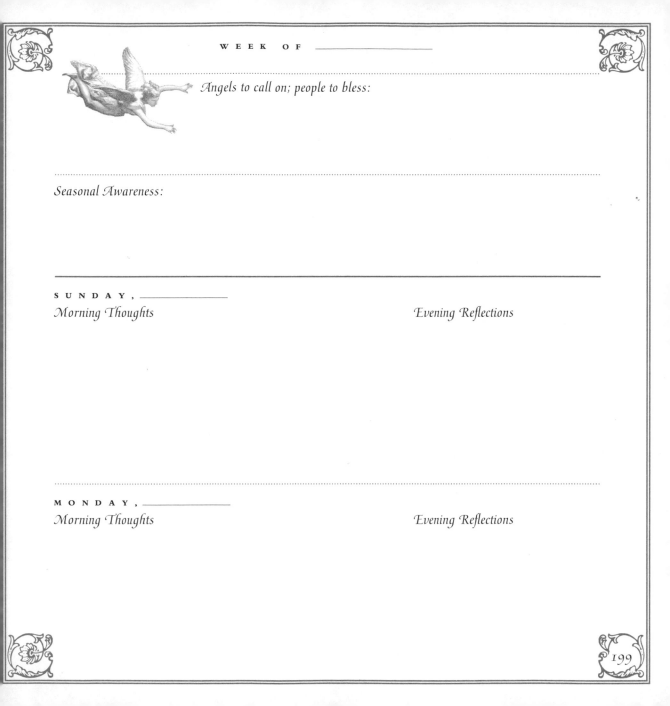

Angels to call on; people to bless:

Seasonal Awareness:

SUNDAY, _____

Morning Thoughts   *Evening Reflections*

MONDAY, _____

Morning Thoughts   *Evening Reflections*

TUESDAY, _____

Morning Thoughts   *Evening Reflections*

WEDNESDAY, _____

Morning Thoughts   *Evening Reflections*

THURSDAY, _____

Morning Thoughts   *Evening Reflections*

FRIDAY, _____
Morning Thoughts   *Evening Reflections*

SATURDAY, _____
Morning Thoughts   *Evening Reflections*

Thoughts About the Week:

Artist

*W*e are attracted to artists because their search for truth requires innate bravery—the courage to expand and evolve. To enjoy life deeply you must become a life-artist in your own special way. The angels exist to help us accomplish this. Within each of our souls lies the seed of a true artist waiting to respond to life as an empty canvas waits to reflect beauty.

DO IT

- *Become an artist in your own way. Each hour, do one thing that you imagine an artist would do.*
- *Become intoxicated by beauty.*
- *Watch the clouds for angel art.*
- *Become a free spirit.*

Goals:

Prayer requests
or notes to your
highest angel:

Concerns, worries,
fears to overcome:

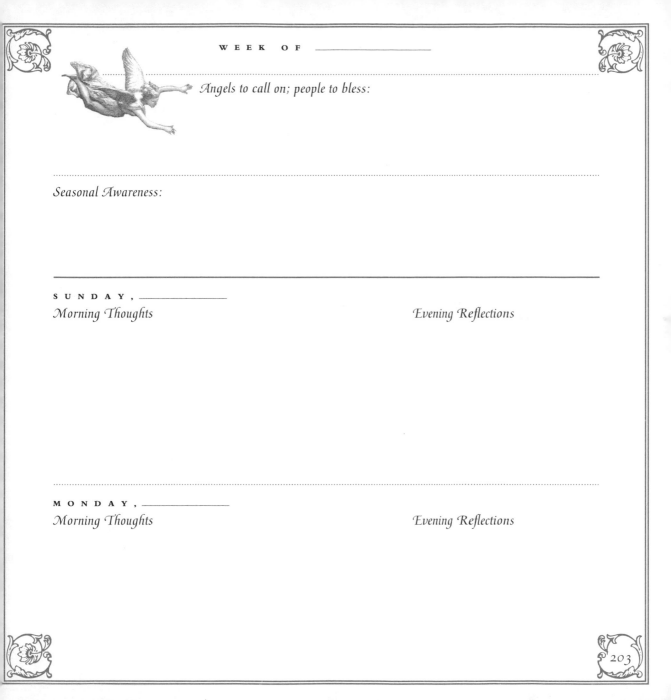

Angels to call on; people to bless:

Seasonal Awareness:

SUNDAY , _____
Morning Thoughts   *Evening Reflections*

MONDAY , _____
Morning Thoughts   *Evening Reflections*

TUESDAY, _____

Morning Thoughts   *Evening Reflections*

WEDNESDAY, _____

Morning Thoughts   *Evening Reflections*

THURSDAY, _____

Morning Thoughts   *Evening Reflections*

FRIDAY, _____

Morning Thoughts   *Evening Reflections*

SATURDAY, _____

Morning Thoughts   *Evening Reflections*

Thoughts About the Week:

Happiness

*T*he concept of happiness can make us uneasy if it reminds us of all that we lack. Instead, we must recognize and be grateful for all that we do have, such as the power to be happy regardless of circumstances. Happiness is part of the soul. The more we understand how the angels help us appreciate who we are, the happier we will be, and the more happiness we will have stored for a rainy day.

BE HAPPY, CULTIVATE HAPPINESS

- *Instead of overreacting to situations, respond without judging or comparing.*
- *Make others happy.*
- *Be willing to give up control over situations that cause you worry.*
- *Stop behaving like a robot or automaton; life is to be experienced.*
- *Know the angels as happiness trainers.*
- *Happiness can only happen now: past happiness is spent, future happiness is out of our reach.*

Goals:

Prayer requests
or notes to your
highest angel:

Concerns, worries,
fears to overcome:

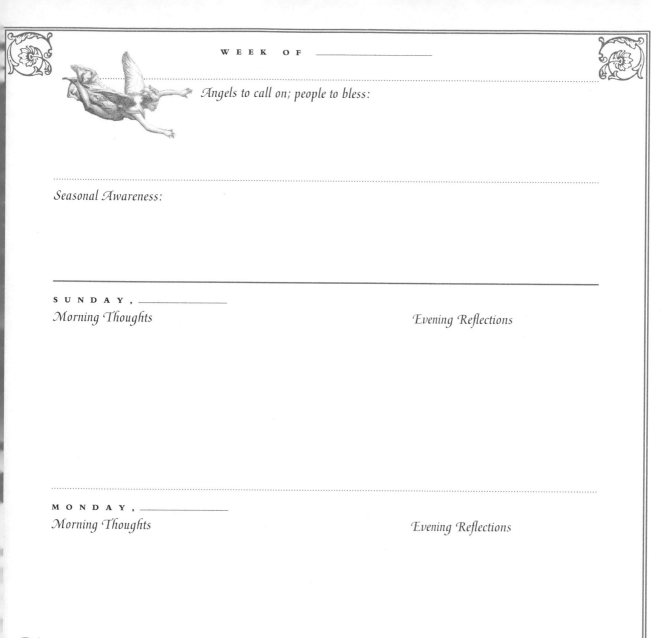

WEEK OF _____

Angels to call on; people to bless:

Seasonal Awareness:

S U N D A Y , _____
Morning Thoughts   *Evening Reflections*

M O N D A Y , _____
Morning Thoughts   *Evening Reflections*

TUESDAY, _____

Morning Thoughts   *Evening Reflections*

WEDNESDAY, _____

Morning Thoughts   *Evening Reflections*

THURSDAY, _____

Morning Thoughts   *Evening Reflections*

FRIDAY, _____
Morning Thoughts   *Evening Reflections*

SATURDAY, _____
Morning Thoughts   *Evening Reflections*

Thoughts About the Week:

Flexibility

*F*lexible means capable of bending. A flexible person is an adaptable, creative person who doesn't freeze in the face of change. Flexibility calls for substance and discipline. If we are too flexible we will be like a loose string on a musical instrument—a string that can't be played. If we are not flexible enough we will be strung so tightly we may snap.

CONTEMPLATION

Flexibility hatches strength.
I am willing to bend and stretch
to find new paths of understanding.
When my creative energy surges, I
will flex in harmony and live in tune with the angels.

Goals:

Prayer requests
or notes to your
highest angel:

Concerns, worries,
fears to overcome:

WEEK OF _____

Angels to call on; people to bless:

Seasonal Awareness:

SUNDAY, _____

Morning Thoughts   *Evening Reflections*

MONDAY, _____

Morning Thoughts   *Evening Reflections*

TUESDAY, _____
Morning Thoughts   *Evening Reflections*

WEDNESDAY, _____
Morning Thoughts   *Evening Reflections*

THURSDAY, _____
Morning Thoughts   *Evening Reflections*

FRIDAY, _____

Morning Thoughts   *Evening Reflections*

....

SATURDAY, _____

Morning Thoughts   *Evening Reflections*

_____

Thoughts About the Week:

Humility

*I*f there is a key to greatness, it has to be humility. Humility is a combination of awareness, modesty, gratitude, and grace. When we recognize our talents and our abilities but do not identify solely with the position that may go along with them, we are humble. True humility means we are always grateful to a higher source of power and wisdom for our gifts and talents. The angels vibrate to the high note of humility.

HUMILITY CANNOT BE FAKED

- *When you are busy living your life and finding ways to make the Earth a more people-friendly place, humility becomes a natural trait. When given a compliment, honor the Divine in yourself and in the person who has recognized you in this way, for the Divine exists in all of us.*
- *Humility means we can laugh at ourselves in the moment of our mistakes. Know the difference between hubris and being proud of your accomplishments.*

Goals:

Prayer requests
or notes to your
highest angel:

Concerns, worries,
fears to overcome:

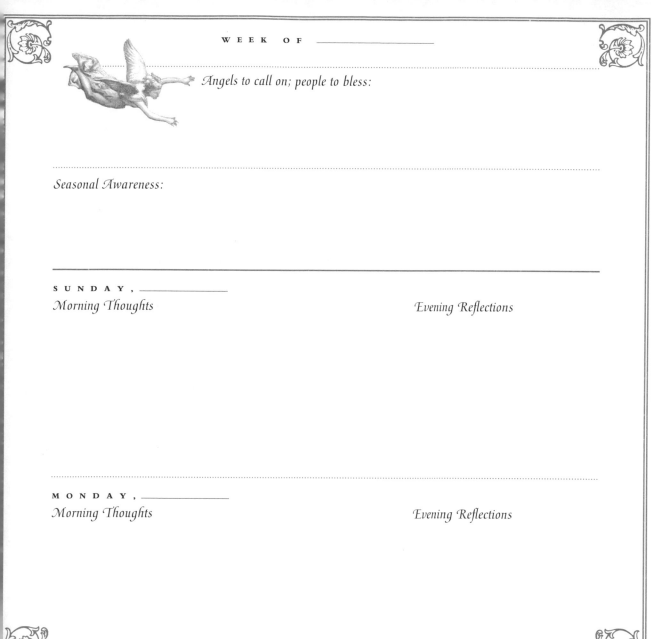

WEEK OF _____

Angels to call on; people to bless:

Seasonal Awareness:

SUNDAY, _____

Morning Thoughts   *Evening Reflections*

MONDAY, _____

Morning Thoughts   *Evening Reflections*

WEEK OF _____

TUESDAY, _____
Morning Thoughts   *Evening Reflections*

WEDNESDAY, _____
Morning Thoughts   *Evening Reflections*

THURSDAY, _____
Morning Thoughts   *Evening Reflections*

WEEK OF _____

FRIDAY, _____

Morning Thoughts   *Evening Reflections*

SATURDAY, _____

Morning Thoughts   *Evening Reflections*

Thoughts About the Week:

WEEK OF _____

ANGELIC SPIRIT OF THE WEEK

Champion

A champion is a winner. To be a champion does not mean you have to compete, but it does mean that you must play the game of your own life. You must be an active player and care deeply for others. We can help champion others to greatness, just as the angels do for us.

CONTEMPLATION

I have angels who are my champions.
They defend and protect me.
With the angels in my life I can be a champion
for others and for myself.
I know that the true spirit of winning comes from
inner strength and peace.

Goals:

Prayer requests
or notes to your
highest angel:

Concerns, worries,
fears to overcome:

218

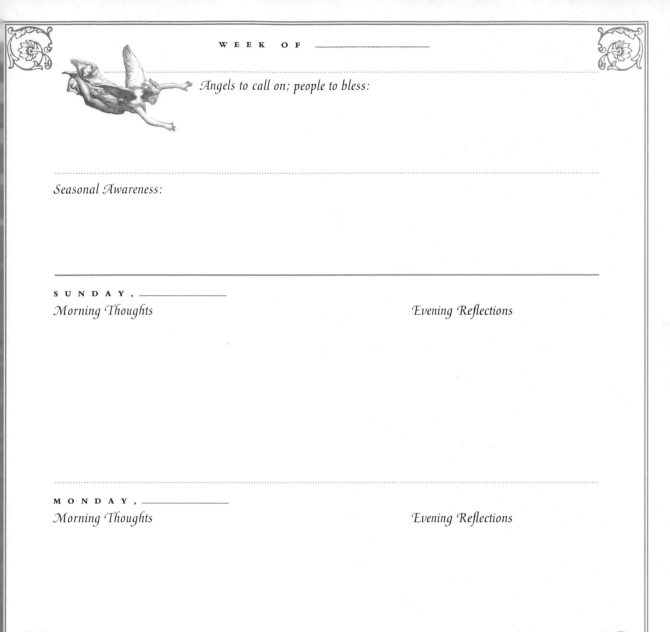

WEEK OF _____

Angels to call on; people to bless:

Seasonal Awareness:

SUNDAY, _____
Morning Thoughts   *Evening Reflections*

MONDAY, _____
Morning Thoughts   *Evening Reflections*

TUESDAY, _____

Morning Thoughts   *Evening Reflections*

WEDNESDAY, _____

Morning Thoughts   *Evening Reflections*

THURSDAY, _____

Morning Thoughts   *Evening Reflections*

FRIDAY, _____

Morning Thoughts   *Evening Reflections*

SATURDAY, _____

Morning Thoughts   *Evening Reflections*

Thoughts About the Week:

ANGELIC SPIRIT OF THE WEEK

Light

Light is often used to represent consciousness. Light is a current, an energy; it needs a system to flow through. Light has a current of frequency referring to the number of complete cycles of a wave that occur within a period of time. High frequency would mean bright light is generated; lower frequency would mean dimmer, or less light.

LIGHTEN YOUR THINKING

- *Thoughts and emotions can be perceived as carrying a frequency of light. Thoughts or emotions that create fear have a lower frequency and are draining. Thoughts and emotions that create love energize and have a higher frequency.*
- *Think about enlightening your mind. What can you do to move toward an enlightened state?*

Goals:

Prayer requests
or notes to your
highest angel:

Concerns, worries,
fears to overcome:

Angels to call on; people to bless:

Seasonal Awareness:

SUNDAY, _____

Morning Thoughts   *Evening Reflections*

MONDAY, _____

Morning Thoughts   *Evening Reflections*

T U E S D A Y , _____

Morning Thoughts

Evening Reflections

W E D N E S D A Y , _____

Morning Thoughts

Evening Reflections

T H U R S D A Y , _____

Morning Thoughts

Evening Reflections

FRIDAY, _____
Morning Thoughts   *Evening Reflections*

SATURDAY, _____
Morning Thoughts   *Evening Reflections*

Thoughts About the Week:

Enthusiasm

W hen you are enthusiastic, you are filled with God. The angels are pure enthusiasm, vibrating at such a high point that the least little connection with the angels fills us with God. The best thing we can do is to be enthusiastic about life and all things that affirm truth and beauty.

CONTEMPLATION

I am filled with God.
I am made from the light.
The angels know me.
How can I not be moved to love deeply
the life I have been given?
I will travel the path of true willingness.

Goals:

Prayer requests
or notes to your
highest angel:

Concerns, worries,
fears to overcome:

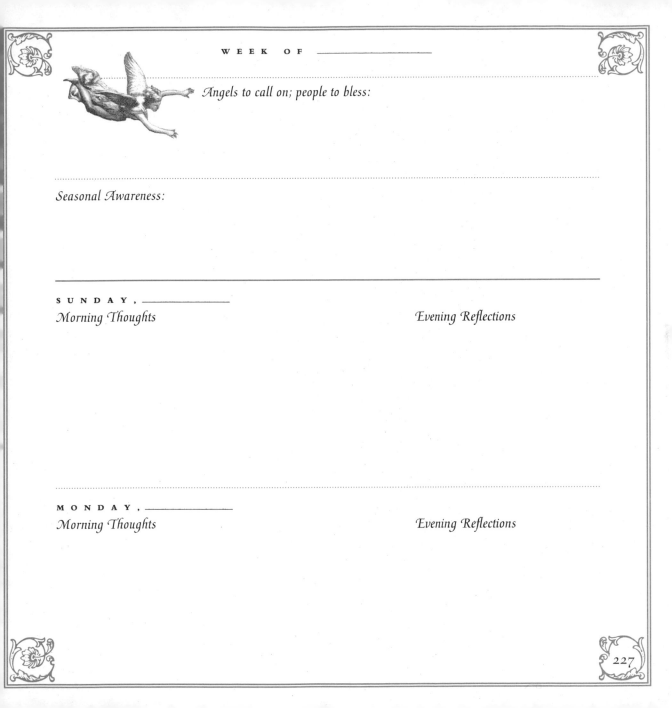

WEEK OF _____

Angels to call on; people to bless:

Seasonal Awareness:

SUNDAY, _____
Morning Thoughts   *Evening Reflections*

MONDAY, _____
Morning Thoughts   *Evening Reflections*

TUESDAY, _____

Morning Thoughts   *Evening Reflections*

WEDNESDAY, _____

Morning Thoughts   *Evening Reflections*

THURSDAY, _____

Morning Thoughts   *Evening Reflections*

FRIDAY, _____

Morning Thoughts   *Evening Reflections*

SATURDAY, _____

Morning Thoughts   *Evening Reflections*

Thoughts About the Week:

Presence

P resence is the state of being consciously aware of ourselves. It is an aura we create and carry with us. To be great, you must have a presence that embodies self-respect and confidence. You must accept the fact that you are worthy to occupy space, worthy to feel loved, and worthy of attention from the angels.

A S K   Y O U R S E L F

- *Is my energy scattered?*
- *Am I centered and able to direct my energy and attention for the highest good?*
- *What do I carry around—sparkling light, open heart, humor?*
- *What is my presence transmitting right now?*

Goals:

*Prayer requests
or notes to your
highest angel:*

*Concerns, worries,
fears to overcome:*

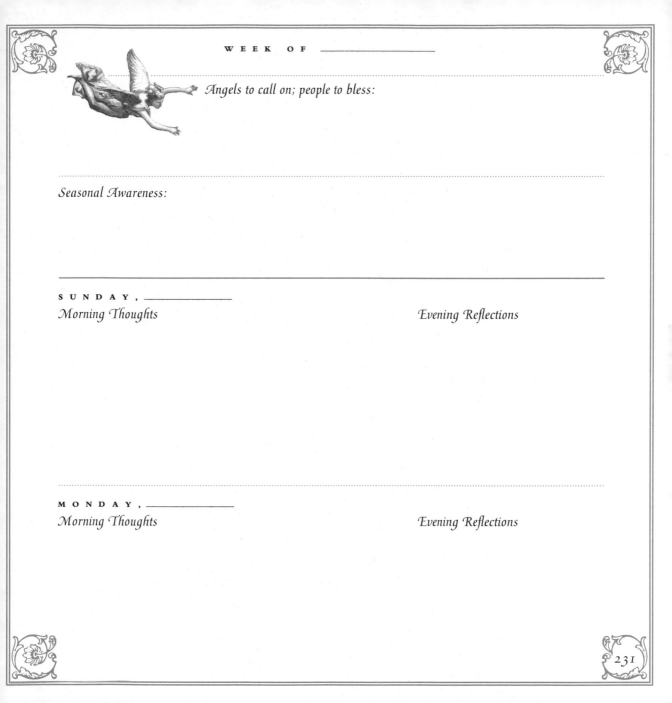

WEEK OF _____

Angels to call on; people to bless:

Seasonal Awareness:

SUNDAY, _____

Morning Thoughts   *Evening Reflections*

MONDAY, _____

Morning Thoughts   *Evening Reflections*

TUESDAY, _____
Morning Thoughts   *Evening Reflections*

WEDNESDAY, _____
Morning Thoughts   *Evening Reflections*

THURSDAY, _____
Morning Thoughts   *Evening Reflections*

FRIDAY, _____

Morning Thoughts   *Evening Reflections*

SATURDAY, _____

Morning Thoughts   *Evening Reflections*

Thoughts About the Week:

Mindfulness

A mind is a space that is always in the process of filling itself up, then emptying itself out. We can choose what we will allow to fill our minds. The farther away we go from habitual thought patterns, the more our minds will be filled with beautiful sensations and responses to life. When we are mindful of the angels, we have a life full of love and beauty.

CONTEMPLATION

I notice subtleties, I watch without words.
Everything has a voice that I recognize.
I walk inside the breezes and the scents.
Every stimulus enlarges my experience.
I am mindful of each moment, body, mind, soul, and spirit.
My mind is full of angels.

Goals:

....

Prayer requests
or notes to your
highest angel:

....

Concerns, worries,
fears to overcome:

WEEK OF _____

Angels to call on; people to bless:

Seasonal Awareness:

SUNDAY, _____

Morning Thoughts   *Evening Reflections*

MONDAY, _____

Morning Thoughts   *Evening Reflections*

TUESDAY, _____
Morning Thoughts   Evening Reflections

WEDNESDAY, _____
Morning Thoughts   Evening Reflections

THURSDAY, _____
Morning Thoughts   Evening Reflections

WEEK OF _____

FRIDAY, _____

Morning Thoughts   *Evening Reflections*

SATURDAY, _____

Morning Thoughts   *Evening Reflections*

Thoughts About the Week:

237

ANGELIC SPIRIT OF THE WEEK

Healing

Life is really a journey of healing ourselves, becoming whole. At times you may not like or even want your whole life; but if you try to cut off part of it you have stopped healing, for healing means to make whole again. Healing is not always about curing a disease. Healing is sometimes about learning to accept a disease, and a not-so-perfect body, and realizing how dear life really is.

PEACE

- *Healing means we have found a quiet joy in knowing that God and the angels are with us every little step of the way, even and especially when we don't feel their nearness.*
- *Healing is making peace with the impermanence of life and knowing this brings greatness.*
- *The angels heal us through beauty and truth, on levels we must not question.*

Goals:

*Prayer requests
or notes to your
highest angel:*

*Concerns, worries,
fears to overcome:*

WEEK OF _____

Angels to call on; people to bless:

Seasonal Awareness:

SUNDAY, _____
Morning Thoughts   *Evening Reflections*

MONDAY, _____
Morning Thoughts   *Evening Reflections*

TUESDAY, _____

Morning Thoughts   *Evening Reflections*

WEDNESDAY, _____

Morning Thoughts   *Evening Reflections*

THURSDAY, _____

Morning Thoughts   *Evening Reflections*

FRIDAY, _____

Morning Thoughts   *Evening Reflections*

SATURDAY, _____

Morning Thoughts   *Evening Reflections*

Thoughts About the Week:

Destiny

I t does not matter if one believes in destiny. Destiny does not depend on a human's belief, it just is. All that you are now is your destiny. Your response to life shapes your destiny. Whom you share time with will color your destiny. Share your destiny with the angels and all will be well fated.

CONTEMPLATION

Mysterious destiny.
Are we living backwards?
Is fate our kind sister, or harsh jailer?
Is everything predetermined?
Are we mere pawns in a merciless game?
When our destiny is Heaven, and our guides the angels,
we are always in the perfect place at the right time.

Goals:

Prayer requests
or notes to your
highest angel:

Concerns, worries,
fears to overcome:

Angels to call on; people to bless:

Seasonal Awareness:

SUNDAY, _____
Morning Thoughts   *Evening Reflections*

MONDAY, _____
Morning Thoughts   *Evening Reflections*

....

TUESDAY, _____

Morning Thoughts   *Evening Reflections*

....

WEDNESDAY, _____

Morning Thoughts   *Evening Reflections*

....

THURSDAY, _____

Morning Thoughts   *Evening Reflections*

FRIDAY, _____

Morning Thoughts   *Evening Reflections*

SATURDAY, _____

Morning Thoughts   *Evening Reflections*

Thoughts About the Week:

ANGELIC SPIRIT OF THE WEEK

Patience

*I*f the word *patience* gives you a pang of anxiety, then it is time to invent a new way to be patient. Patience by definition is calm endurance, tolerance, and understanding. For patience to turn into magic, it has to be comfortable and peaceful. Often we need to wait for things to unfold gloriously and to take time to listen to the angels. Good things come to those who wait to accept them with a grateful heart.

PLAY A LITTLE GAME WITH THE ANGELS

Each time you think about that for which you are waiting, imagine that the angels are saying to you (or say to yourself), "patience." When you hear it in your mind, immediately allow a sense of calm to come over you. As you take a deep breath, feel your shoulders relax and your breath expand deep into your solar plexus. On the exhale say in your mind, "patience." Practice using the word patience *as a signal to relax and trust the angels.*

Goals:

Prayer requests
or notes to your
highest angel:

Concerns, worries,
fears to overcome:

Angels to call on; people to bless:

Seasonal Awareness:

S U N D A Y , _____
Morning Thoughts   *Evening Reflections*

M O N D A Y , _____
Morning Thoughts   *Evening Reflections*

TUESDAY, _____

Morning Thoughts   *Evening Reflections*

WEDNESDAY, _____

Morning Thoughts   *Evening Reflections*

THURSDAY, _____

Morning Thoughts   *Evening Reflections*

WEEK OF _____

FRIDAY, _____

Morning Thoughts   *Evening Reflections*

SATURDAY, _____

Morning Thoughts   *Evening Reflections*

Thoughts About the Week:

Cheer

*C*heer is anything that brings us happiness and comfort. Cheer produces a sense of gaiety that can lead to an angelic state of mirth. When we cheer others on, we provide encouragement and congratulation. The angels have a special way of cheering us on to be our best selves.

CONTEMPLATION

My spirits are naturally high.
Happiness is a peaceful river that flows in my life
forever offering cheer and comfort.
The angels are the cheerleaders of my soul and spirit.
I hear their cheers when I play the game of life
with spirit, passion, and creativity.

Goals:

Prayer requests
or notes to your
highest angel:

Concerns, worries,
fears to overcome:

Angels to call on; people to bless:

Seasonal Awareness:

S U N D A Y , _____

Morning Thoughts   *Evening Reflections*

M O N D A Y , _____

Morning Thoughts   *Evening Reflections*

TUESDAY, _____

Morning Thoughts   *Evening Reflections*

WEDNESDAY, _____

Morning Thoughts   *Evening Reflections*

THURSDAY, _____

Morning Thoughts   *Evening Reflections*

FRIDAY, _____

Morning Thoughts   *Evening Reflections*

SATURDAY, _____

Morning Thoughts   *Evening Reflections*

Thoughts About the Week:

253

ANGELIC SPIRIT OF THE WEEK

Choice

*I*t becomes clear that at some point we must make a choice whether really to start living, or just to resign ourselves to some meager existence and slowly die in spirit, mind, and body. There are certain death traps we may get into, such as stale relationships, work situations, and identity issues. However, with the angels as our companions through life, if we choose to live fully, we can release ourselves from the death traps and transform them into vehicles for growth.

CHOOSE LIFE!

- *When we choose life with the angels our hearts grow younger every day. Time doesn't mean the same thing as it does in the "tick-tock world." We realize we have plenty of time to enjoy life; we know what we want to do and we take time to do it.*
- *A trip to the grocery store when you are really alive can be more exciting and give you more stories to tell than some people will have coming home from an exotic vacation.*

Goals:

Prayer requests
or notes to your
highest angel:

Concerns, worries,
fears to overcome:

Angels to call on; people to bless:

Seasonal Awareness:

S U N D A Y , _____
Morning Thoughts   *Evening Reflections*

M O N D A Y , _____
Morning Thoughts   *Evening Reflections*

....

T U E S D A Y , _____

Morning Thoughts   *Evening Reflections*

....

W E D N E S D A Y , _____

Morning Thoughts   *Evening Reflections*

....

T H U R S D A Y , _____

Morning Thoughts   *Evening Reflections*

FRIDAY , _____

Morning Thoughts   *Evening Reflections*

SATURDAY , _____

Morning Thoughts   *Evening Reflections*

Thoughts About the Week:

Recommended Reading

SEASONS AND ARCHANGELS

Anderson, Adrian. *Living a Spiritual Year*. Hudson, NY: Anthroposophic Press, 1993.

Andrews, Ted. *The Occult Christ, Angelic Mysteries, Seasonal Rituals, and the Divine Feminine*. St. Paul: Llewellyn Publications, 1993.

Heline, Corinne. *Star Gates*. Santa Monica, CA: New Age Press, 1986.

Steiner, Rudolf. *The Four Seasons and the Archangels*. Bristol, England: Rudolf Steiner Press, 1992.

JOURNALING, WRITING, CREATIVITY

Baldwin, Christina. *Life's Companion: Journal Writing as a Spiritual Quest.* New York: Bantam, 1990.

Metzger, Deena. *Writing for Your Life.* San Francisco: Harper, 1992.

Rainer, Tristine. *The New Diary.* Los Angeles: J. P. Tarcher, 1978.

Taylor, Terry Lynn. *Creating with the Angels.* Tiburon, CA: H. J. Kramer, 1993.

Acknowledgments

I thank Karyn Martin-Kuri for providing the inspiration, information, and years of expertise for the seasonal angel information. She is a valued friend and teacher and provided a much-needed source of support and guidance while I pulled this project together.

Lorretta Barrett, my angelic agent, is a true blessing in my life and I thank her for her vision, strength, and friendship.

Joëlle Delbourgo is the foremost mover and shaker of the angel consciousness movement. She had the vision in the beginning to see where the angels are taking humans and has been responsible for many brilliant writings and insights that have changed many lives. I thank her for the honor of providing this book and for her support and keen executive editing skills. Thanks also to Lesley Malin Helm, who came in to shape and sculpt this project, for her enthusiastic support and editing.

And thanks to all of you who keep angel consciousness alive and well—thank you for your letters and for touching my heart through your support and good wishes!

If you would like to contact Terry Lynn Taylor, you may write to her at:

2275 Huntington Drive
#326
San Marino, CA 91108

To obtain her newsletter and catalog of tapes and other angel-related
items, please send a self-addressed, stamped envelope to the above address.

PHOTO CREDITS

FRONTISPIECE

Three Angels, *detail from* The Adoration of the Virgin,
by Perugino, fifteenth century, Art Resource, NY.

PAGE 22

Michael, *by Raphael, Art Resource, NY.*

PAGE 28

Gabriel, *by Filippo Lippi, Art Resource, NY.*

PAGE 34

Tobias and the Angel, *by Filippino Lippi,*
National Gallery of Art, Washington.

PAGE 40

Uriel and Jacob, *from* The Doré Bible Illustrations, *by Gustave Doré.*